Bernie Speaks

Greenbridge Publishing

BERNIE SPEAKS

"*The political revolution is not about one election or one candidate. It is about transforming America and continuing the fight for economic, social, racial and environmental justice. We have to continue to work together to advance the progressive future we all support.*"

BERNIE SANDERS

"I fear very much that, in fact, government of the people, by the people and for the people is beginning to perish in America."

BERNIE SANDERS

BERNIE SANDERS

Table of Contents

BERNIE SANDERS

CHAPTER 1
Westminster College Address
September 21, 2017

Let me begin by thanking Westminster College, which year after year invites political leaders to discuss the important issue of foreign policy and America's role in the world. I am honored to be here today and I thank you very much for the invitation.

One of the reasons I accepted the invitation to speak here is that I strongly believe that not only do we need to begin a more vigorous debate about foreign policy, we also need to broaden our understanding of what foreign policy is.

So let me be clear: Foreign policy is directly related to military policy and has everything to do with almost seven thousand young Americans being killed in Iraq and Afghanistan, and tens of thousands coming home wounded in body and spirit from a war we should never have started. That's foreign policy. And foreign policy is about hundreds of thousands of people in Iraq and Afghanistan dying in that same war.

Foreign policy is about U.S. government budget priorities. At a time when we already spend more on defense than the next 12 nations combined, foreign policy is about authorizing a defense budget of some $700 billion, including a $50 billion increase passed just last week.

Meanwhile, at the exact same time as the President and many of my Republican colleagues want to substantially increase military spending, they want to throw 32 million Americans off of the health insurance they currently have because, supposedly, they are worried about the budget deficit. While greatly increasing military spending they also want to cut education, environmental protection and the needs of children and seniors.

Foreign policy, therefore, is remembering what Dwight D. Eisenhower said as he left office: "In the councils of government, we must guard against the acquisition of unwarranted influence, whether sought or unsought, by the military industrial complex. The potential for the disastrous rise of misplaced power exists and will persist."

And he also reminded us that; "Every gun that is made, every warship launched, every rocket fired signifies, in the final sense, a theft from those who hunger and are not fed, those who are cold and are not clothed. This world in arms is not spending money alone. It is spending the sweat of its laborers, the genius of its scientists, the hopes of its children. The cost of one modern heavy bomber is this: a modern brick school in more than 30 cities. It is two electric power plants, each serving a town of 60,000 population. It is two fine, fully equipped hospitals. It is some 50 miles of concrete highway...."

What Eisenhower said over 50 years ago is even more true today.

Foreign policy is about whether we continue to champion the values of freedom, democracy and justice, values which have been a beacon of hope for people throughout the world, or whether we support undemocratic, repressive regimes, which torture, jail and deny basic rights to their citizens.

What foreign policy also means is that if we are going to expound the virtues of democracy and justice abroad, and be taken seriously, we need to practice those values here at home. That means continuing the struggle to end racism, sexism, xenophobia and homophobia here in the United States and making it clear that when people in America march on our streets as neo-nazis or white supremacists, we have no ambiguity in condemning everything they stand for. There are no two sides on that issue.

Foreign policy is not just tied into military affairs, it is directly connected to economics. Foreign policy must take into account the outrageous income and wealth inequality that exists globally and in our own country. This planet will not be secure or peaceful when so few have so much, and so many have so little – and when we advance day after day into an oligarchic form of society where a small number of extraordinarily powerful special interests exert enormous influence over the economic and political life of the world.

There is no moral or economic justification for the six wealthiest people in the world having as much wealth as the bottom half of the world's population – 3.7 billion people. There is no justification for the incredible power and dominance that Wall Street, giant multi-national corporations and international financial institutions have over the affairs of sovereign countries throughout the world.

At a time when climate change is causing devastating problems here in America and around the world, foreign policy is about whether we work with the international community – with China, Russia, India and countries around the world - to transform our energy systems away from fossil fuel to energy efficiency and sustainable energy. Sensible foreign policy understands that climate change is a real threat to every country on earth, that it is not a hoax, and that no country alone can effectively combat it. It is an issue for the entire international community, and an issue that the United States should be leading in, not ignoring or denying.

My point is that we need to look at foreign policy as more than just the crisis of the day. That is important, but we need a more expansive view.

Almost 70 years ago, former British Prime Minister Winston Churchill stood on this stage and gave an historic address, known as the "Iron Curtain" speech, in which he framed a conception of world affairs that endured through the 20th century, until the collapse of the Soviet Union. In that speech, he defined his strategic concept as quote "nothing less than the safety and welfare, the freedom and progress, of all the homes and families of all the men and women in all the lands."

"To give security to these countless homes," he said, "they must be shielded from the two giant marauders, war and tyranny."

How do we meet that challenge today? How do we fight for the "freedom and progress" that Churchill talked about in the year 2017? At a time of exploding technology and wealth, how do we move away from a world of war, terrorism and massive levels of poverty into a world of peace and economic security for all. How do we move toward a global community in which people have the decent jobs, food, clean water, education, health care and housing they need? These are, admittedly, not easy issues to deal with, but they are questions we cannot afford to ignore.

At the outset, I think it is important to recognize that the world of today is very, very different from the world of Winston Churchill of 1946. Back then we faced a superpower adversary with a huge standing army, with an arsenal of nuclear weapons, with allies around the world, and with expansionist aims. Today the Soviet Union no longer exists.

Today we face threats of a different sort. We will never forget 9/11. We are cognizant of the terrible attacks that have taken place in capitals all over the world. We are more than aware of the brutality of ISIS, Al Qaeda, and similar groups.

We also face the threat of these groups obtaining weapons of mass destruction, and preventing that must be a priority.

In recent years, we are increasingly confronted by the isolated dictatorship of North Korea, which is making rapid progress in nuclear weaponry and intercontinental ballistic missiles.

Yes, we face real and very serious threats to our security, which I will discuss, but they are very different than what we have seen in the past and our response must be equally different.

But before I talk about some of these other

threats, let me say a few words about a very insidious challenge that undermines our ability to meet these other crises, and indeed could undermine our very way of life.

A great concern that I have today is that many in our country are losing faith in our common future and in our democratic values.

For far too many of our people, here in the United States and people all over the world, the promises of self-government -- of government by the people, for the people, and of the people -- have not been kept. And people are losing faith.

In the United States and other countries, a majority of people are working longer hours for lower wages than they used to. They see big money buying elections, and they see a political and economic elite growing wealthier, even as their own children's future grows dimmer.

So when we talk about foreign policy, and our belief in democracy, at the very top of our list of concerns is the need to revitalize American democracy to ensure that governmental decisions reflect the interests of a majority of our people, and not just the few – whether that few is Wall Street, the military industrial complex, or the fossil fuel industry. We cannot convincingly promote democracy abroad if we do not live it vigorously here at home.

Maybe it's because I come from the small state of Vermont, a state that prides itself on town meetings and grassroots democracy, that I strongly agree with Winston Churchill when he stated his belief that "democracy is the worst form of government, except for all those other forms."

In both Europe and the United States, the international order which the United States helped establish over the past 70 years, one which put great emphasis on democracy and human rights, and promoted greater trade and economic development, is under great strain. Many Europeans are questioning the value of the European Union. Many Americans are questioning the value of the United Nations, of the transatlantic alliance, and other multilateral organizations.

We also see a rise in authoritarianism and right wing extremism – both domestic and foreign -- which further weakens this order by exploiting and amplifying resentments, stoking intolerance and fanning ethnic and racial hatreds among those in our societies who are struggling.

We saw this anti-democratic effort take place in the 2016 election right here in the United States, where we now know that the Russian government was engaged in a massive effort to undermine one of our greatest strengths: The integrity of our elections, and our faith in our own democracy.

I found it incredible, by the way, that when the President of the United States spoke before the United Nations on Monday, he did not even mention that outrage.

Well, I will. Today I say to Mr. Putin: we will not allow you to undermine American democracy or democracies around the world. In fact, our goal is to not only strengthen American democracy, but to work in solidarity with supporters of democracy around the globe, including in Russia. In the struggle of democracy versus authoritarianism, we intend to win.

When we talk about foreign policy it is clear that there are some who believe that the United States would be best served by withdrawing from the global community. I disagree. As the wealthiest and most powerful nation on earth, we have got to help lead the struggle to defend and expand a rules-based international order in which law, not might, makes right.

We must offer people a vision that one day, maybe not in our lifetimes, but one day in the future human beings on this planet will live in a world where international conflicts will be resolved peacefully, not by mass murder.

How tragic it is that today, while hundreds of millions of people live in abysmal poverty, the arms merchants of the world grow increasingly rich as governments spend trillions of dollars on weapons of destruction.

I am not naïve or unmindful of history. Many of the conflicts that plague our world are longstanding and complex. But we must never lose our vision of a world in which, to quote the Prophet Isaiah, "they shall beat their swords into plowshares, and their spears into pruning hooks: nation shall not lift up sword against nation, neither shall they learn war any more."

One of the most important organizations for promoting a vision of a different world is the United Nations. Former First Lady Eleanor Roosevelt, who helped create the UN, called it "our greatest hope for future peace. Alone we cannot keep the peace of the world, but in cooperation with others we have to achieve this much longed-for security."

It has become fashionable to bash the UN. And yes, the UN needs to be reformed. It can be ineffective, bureaucratic, too slow or unwilling to act, even in the face of massive atrocities, as we are seeing in Syria right now. But to see only its weaknesses is to overlook the enormously important work the UN does in promoting global health, aiding refugees, monitoring elections, and doing international peacekeeping missions, among other things. All of these activities contribute to reduced conflict, to wars that don't have to be ended because they never start.

At the end of the day, it is obvious that it makes far more sense to have a forum in which countries can debate their concerns, work out compromises and agreements. Dialogue and debate are far preferable to bombs, poison gas, and war.

Dialogue however cannot only be take place between foreign ministers or diplomats at the United Nations. It should be taking place between people throughout the world at the grassroots level.

I was mayor of the city of Burlington, Vermont, in the 1980's, when the Soviet Union was our enemy. We established a sister city program with the Russian city of Yaroslavl, a program which still exists today. I will never forget seeing Russian boys and girls visiting Vermont, getting to know American kids, and becoming good friends. Hatred and wars are often based on fear and ignorance. The way to defeat this ignorance and diminish this fear is through meeting with others and understanding the way they see the world. Good foreign policy means building people to people relationships.

We should welcome young people from all over the world and all walks of life to spend time with our kids in American classrooms, while our kids, from all income levels, do the same abroad.

Some in Washington continue to argue that "benevolent global hegemony" should be the goal of our foreign policy, that the US, by virtue of its extraordinary military power, should stand astride the world and reshape it to its liking. I would argue that the events of the past two decades — particularly the disastrous Iraq war and the instability and destruction it has brought to the region — have utterly discredited that vision.

The goal is not for the United States to dominate the world. Nor, on the other hand, is our goal to withdraw from the international community and shirk our responsibilities under the banner of "America First." Our goal should be global engagement based on partnership, rather than dominance. This is better for our security, better for global stability, and better for facilitating the international cooperation necessary to meet shared challenges.

Here's a truth that you don't often hear about too often in the newspapers, on the television, or in the halls of Congress. But it's a truth we must face. Far too often, American intervention and the use of American military power has produced unintended consequences which have caused incalculable harm. Yes, it is reasonably easy to engineer the overthrow of a government. It is far harder, however, to know the long term impact that that action will have. Let me give you some examples:

In 1953 the United States, on behalf of Western oil interests, supported the overthrow of Iran's elected Prime Minister Mohammed Mossadegh, and the re-installation of the Shah of Iran, who led a corrupt, brutal and unpopular government. In 1979, the Shah was overthrown by revolutionaries led by Ayatollah Khomeini, and the Islamic Republic of Iran was created. What would Iran look like today if their democratic government had not been overthrown? What impact did that American-led coup have on the entire region? What consequences are we still living with today?

In 1973, the United States supported the coup against the democratically elected president of Chile Salvador Allende which was led by General Augusto Pinochet. The result was almost 20 years of authoritarian military rule and the disappearance and torture of thousands of Chileans – and the intensification of anti-Americanism in Latin America.

Elsewhere in Latin America, the logic of the Cold War led the United States to support murderous regimes in El Salvador and Guatemala, which resulted in brutal and long-lasting civil wars that killed hundreds of thousands of innocent men, women and children.

In Vietnam, based on a discredited "domino theory," the United States replaced the French in intervening in a civil war, which resulted in the deaths of millions of Vietnamese in support of a corrupt, repressive South Vietnamese government. We must never forget that over 58,000 thousand Americans also died in that war.

More recently, in Iraq, based on a similarly mistaken analysis of the threat posed by Saddam Hussein's regime, the United States invaded and occupied a country in the heart of the Middle East. In doing so, we upended the regional order of the Middle East and unleashed forces across the region and the world that we'll be dealing with for decades to come.

These are just a few examples of American foreign policy and interventionism which proved to be counter-productive.

Now let me give you an example of an incredibly bold and ambitious American initiative which proved to be enormously successful in which not one bullet was fired — something that we must learn from.

Shortly after Churchill was right here in Westminster College, the United States developed an extremely radical foreign policy initiative called the

Marshall Plan.

Think about it for a moment: historically, when countries won terrible wars, they exacted retribution on the vanquished. But in 1948, the United States government did something absolutely unprecedented.

After losing hundreds of thousands of soldiers in the most brutal war in history to defeat the barbarity of Nazi Germany and Japanese imperialism, the government of the United States decided not to punish and humiliate the losers. Rather, we helped rebuild their economies, spending the equivalent of $130 billion just to reconstruct Western Europe after World War II. We also provided them support to reconstruct democratic societies.

That program was an amazing success. Today Germany, the country of the Holocaust, the country of Hitler's dictatorship, is now a strong democracy and the economic engine of Europe. Despite centuries of hostility, there has not been a major European war since World War II. That is an extraordinary foreign policy success that we have every right to be very proud of.

Unfortunately, today we still have examples of the United States supporting policies that I believe will come back to haunt us. One is the ongoing Saudi war in Yemen.

While we rightly condemn Russian and Iranian support for Bashar al-Assad's slaughter in Syria, the United States continues to support Saudi Arabia's destructive intervention in Yemen, which has killed many thousands of civilians and created a humanitarian crisis in one of the region's poorest countries. Such policies dramatically undermine America's ability to advance a human rights agenda around the world, and empowers authoritarian leaders who insist that our support for those rights and values is not serious.

Let me say a word about some of the shared global challenges that we face today.

First, I would mention climate change. Friends, it is time to get serious on this: Climate change is real and must be addressed with the full weight of American power, attention and resources.

The scientific community is virtually unanimous in telling us that climate change is real, climate change is caused by human activity, and climate change is already causing devastating harm throughout the world. Further, what the scientists tell us is that if we do not act boldly to address the climate crisis, this planet will see more drought, more floods — the recent devastation by Hurricanes Harvey and Irma are good examples — more extreme weather disturbances, more acidification of the ocean, more rising sea levels, and, as a result of mass migrations, there will be more threats to global stability and security.

President Trump's decision to withdraw from the Paris agreement was not only incredibly foolish and short-sighted, but it will also end up hurting the American economy.

The threat of climate change is a very clear example of where American leadership can make a difference. Europe can't do it alone, China can't do it alone, and the United States can't do it alone. This is a crisis that calls out for strong international cooperation if we are to leave our children and grandchildren a planet that is healthy and habitable. American leadership — the economic and scientific advantages and incentives that only America can offer — is hugely important for facilitating this cooperation.

Another challenge that we and the entire world face is growing wealth and income inequality, and the movement toward international oligarchy — a system in which a small number of billionaires and corporate interests have control over our economic life, our political life, and our media.

This movement toward oligarchy is not just an American issue. It is an international issue. Globally, the top 1 percent now owns more wealth than the bottom 99% of the world's population.

In other words, while the very, very rich become much richer, thousands of children die every week in poor countries around the world from easily prevented diseases, and hundreds of millions live in incredible squalor.

Inequality, corruption, oligarchy and authoritarianism are inseparable. They must be understood as part of the same system, and fought in the same way. Around the world we have witnessed the rise of demagogues who once in power use their positions to loot the state of its resources. These kleptocrats, like Putin in Russia, use divisiveness and abuse as a tool for enriching themselves and those loyal to them.

But economic inequality is not the only form of inequality that we must face. As we seek to renew America's commitment to promote human rights and human dignity around the world we must be a living example here at home. We must reject the divisive attacks based on a person's religion, race, gender, sexual orientation or identity, country of origin, or class. And when we see demonstrations of neo naziism and white supremacism as we recently did in Charlottesville, Virginia, we must be unequivocal in our condemnation, as our president shamefully was not.

And as we saw here so clearly in St. Louis in the past week we need serious reforms in policing and the criminal justice system so that the life of every person is equally valued and protected. We cannot speak with the moral authority the world needs if we do not struggle to achieve the ideal we are holding out for others.

One of the places we have fallen short in upholding these ideas is in the war on terrorism. Here I want to be clear: terrorism is a very real threat, as we learned so tragically on September 11, 2001, and many other countries knew already too well.

But, I also want to be clear about something else: As an organizing framework, the Global War on Terror has been a disaster for the American people and for American leadership. Orienting US national security strategy around terrorism essentially allowed a few thousand violent extremists to dictate policy for the most powerful nation on earth. It responds to terrorists by giving them exactly what they want.

In addition to draining our resources and distorting our vision, the war on terror has caused us to undermine our own moral standards regarding torture, indefinite detention, and the use of force around the world, using drone strikes and other airstrikes that often result in high civilian casualties.

A heavy-handed military approach, with little

transparency or accountability, doesn't enhance our security. It makes the problem worse.

We must rethink the old Washington mindset that judges "seriousness" according to the willingness to use force. One of the key misapprehensions of this mindset is the idea that military force is decisive in a way that diplomacy is not.

Yes, military force is sometimes necessary, but always — always — as the last resort. And blustery threats of force, while they might make a few columnists happy, can often signal weakness as much as strength, diminishing US deterrence, credibility and security in the process.

To illustrate this, I would contrast two recent US foreign policy initiatives: The Iraq war and the Iran nuclear agreement.

Today it is now broadly acknowledged that the war in Iraq, which I opposed, was a foreign policy blunder of enormous magnitude.

In addition to the many thousands killed, it created a cascade of instability around the region that we are still dealing with today in Syria and elsewhere, and will be for many years to come. Indeed, had it not been for the Iraq War, ISIS would almost certainly not exist.

The Iraq war, as I said before, had unintended consequences. It was intended as a demonstration of the extent of American power. It ended up demonstrating only its limits.

In contrast, the Iran nuclear deal advanced the security of the US and its partners, and it did this at a cost of no blood and zero treasure.

For many years, leaders across the world had become increasingly concerned about the possibility of an Iranian nuclear weapon. What the Obama administration and our European allies were able to do was to get an agreement that froze and dismantled large parts of that nuclear program, put it under the most intensive inspections regime in history, and removed the prospect of an Iranian nuclear weapon from the list of global threats.

That is real leadership. That is real power.

Just yesterday, the top general of US Strategic Command, General John Hyden, said "The facts are that Iran is operating under the agreements the we signed up for." We now have a four-year record of Iran's compliance, going back to the 2013 interim deal.

I call on my colleagues in the Congress, and all Americans: We must protect this deal. President Trump has signaled his intention to walk away from it, as he did the Paris agreement, regardless of the evidence that it is working. That would be a mistake.

Not only would this potentially free Iran from the limits placed on its nuclear program, it would irreparably harm America's ability to negotiate future nonproliferation agreements. Why would any country in the world sign such an agreement with the United States if they knew that a reckless president and an irresponsible Congress might simply discard that agreement a few years later?

If we are genuinely concerned with Iran's behavior in the region, as I am, the worst possible thing we could do is break the nuclear deal. It would make all of these other problems harder.

Another problem it would make harder is that of North Korea.

Let's understand: North Korea is ruled by one of the worst regimes in the world. For many years, its leadership has sacrificed the well-being of its own people in order to develop nuclear weapons and missile programs in order to protect the Kim family's regime. Their continued development of nuclear weapons and missile capability is a growing threat to the US and our allies. Despite past efforts they have repeatedly shown their determination to move forward with these programs in defiance of virtually unanimous international opposition and condemnation.

As we saw with the 2015 nuclear agreement with Iran, real US leadership is shown by our ability to develop consensus around shared problems, and mobilize that consensus toward a solution. That is the model we should be pursuing with North Korea.

As we did with Iran, if North Korea continues to refuse to negotiate seriously, we should look for ways to tighten international sanctions. This will involve working closely with other countries, particularly China, on whom North Korea relies for some 80 percent of its trade. But we should also continue to make clear that this is a shared problem, not to be solved by any one country alone but by the international community working together.

An approach that really uses all the tools of our power — political, economic, civil society — to encourage other states to adopt more inclusive governance will ultimately make us safer.

Development aid is not charity, it advances our national security. It's worth noting that the U.S. military is a stalwart supporter of non-defense diplomacy and development aid.

Starving diplomacy and aid now will result in greater defense needs later on.

US foreign aid should be accompanied by stronger emphasis on helping people gain their political and civil rights to hold oppressive governments accountable to the people. Ultimately, governments that are accountable to the needs of their people will make more dependable partners.

Here is the bottom line: In my view, the United States must seek partnerships not just between governments, but between peoples. A sensible and effective foreign policy recognizes that our safety and welfare is bound up with the safety and welfare of others around the world, with "all the homes and families of all the men and women in all the lands," as Churchill said right here, 70 years ago.

In my view, every person on this planet shares a common humanity. We all want our children to grow up healthy, to have a good education, have decent jobs, drink clean water and breathe clean air, and to live in peace. That's what being human is about.

Our job is to build on that common humanity and do everything that we can to oppose all of the forces, whether unaccountable government power or unaccountable corporate power, who try to divide us up and set us against each other. As Eleanor Roosevelt reminded us, "The world of the future is in our making. Tomorrow is now."

My friends, let us go forward and build that tomorrow.

CHAPTER 2
Brooklyn College
Commencement

May 30, 2017

You know and I know that these are tough times for our country. But I do want to say that standing up here and looking out at the beautiful people in front of me, I have enormous confidence in the future of our country.

Let me begin by congratulating the graduating class of 2017. Today is an important day in your lives, something that I know you have worked very hard to achieve, and I want to wish all of you the very best of luck in your future endeavors.

I do want, on behalf of my wife, Jane, and myself, to pray that you all live healthy and happy lives, doing the work you enjoy surrounded in love by family and friends.

Let me thank President Michelle Anderson, Nicole Haas, the Brooklyn College Administration, faculty and staff and all of you for inviting Jane and me back to Brooklyn where we were both born and raised. am greatly honored of the honorary degree you have given me.

I grew up in Flatbush and, like Senator Schumer, graduated from James Madison High School. My wife, Jane, was also raised Flatbush and Bedford-Stuyvesant, and graduated from St. Savior's High School a few miles away from here.

In 1959, as a first-generation college student I attended Brooklyn College for a year — a year which had a major impact in my life. After that year I left for the University of Chicago, where I eventually graduated. My mom had died the previous year and I felt it was time to leave the neighborhood and see what the rest of the world looked like.

My childhood in Brooklyn was shaped by two profound realities. First, my mom, dad and older brother, who graduated from Brooklyn College, lived in a 3 1/2 room rent-controlled apartment. As with many of your families who don't have a lot of money, financial pressures caused friction and tension within our household. From those experiences of growing up without a lot of money, I have never forgotten that there are millions of people throughout this country who struggle to put food on the table, pay the electric bill, try to save for their kids' education or for retirement — people who against great odds are fighting today to live in dignity.

The second reality that impacted my life was that my father left Poland at the age of 17 from a community which was not only very poor, but from a country where anti-Semitism, pogroms and attacks on Jews were not uncommon. While my father emigrated to the United States, and escaped Hitler and the holocaust, many in his family did not. For them, racism, right-wing extremism and ultra-nationalism were not "political issues." They were issues of life and death — and some of them died horrific deaths

From that experience, what was indelibly stamped on my mind was the understanding that we must never allow demagogues to divide us up by race, by religion, by national origin, by gender or sexual orientation. Black, white, Latino, Asian American, Native American, Christian, Jew, Muslim and every religion, straight or gay, male or female, we must stand together. This country belongs to all of us.

As a United States senator from Vermont let me give you a very brief overview of some of the serious crises we currently face — crises which do not often get attention they deserve.

As a student at James Madison High School, many years ago, I recall my social studies teacher talking about how there were small developing countries around the world that were "oligarchic" societies —places where the economic and political life of the nation were controlled by a handful of very wealthy people. It never occurred to me as a kid in

Brooklyn that the United States of America, our great nation, could move in that direction. But that is precisely, in my view, what is happening today.

Today, the top 1/10 of 1% now owns almost as much wealth as the bottom 90%. Twenty Americans now own as much wealth as the bottom half of America and one family now owns more wealth than the bottom 42 percent of our people. In the last 17 years, while the middle class continues to decline, we have seen a tenfold increase in the number of billionaires. Today in America CEOs are earning almost 350 times more than the average worker makes. In terms of income, while you and your parents are working in some cases two or three jobs, 52 % of all new income goes to the top 1%.

At the same time as we have more income and wealth inequality than any other major nation, 43 million Americans live in poverty, we have the highest rate of childhood poverty of almost any major country in earth, half of older workers have nothing in the bank as they approach retirement and in some inner cities and rural communities, youth unemployment is 20, 30, 40%. Unbelievably, in our country today as a result of hopelessness and despair we are seeing a decline in life expectancy. People are giving up. And they're turning to drugs, to alcohol, and even to suicide. And because of poverty, racism today in a broken criminal justice system we have more people in jail than any other country on Earth. Those people are disproportionately black, Latino and Native American.

Directly related to the oligarchic economy that we currently have is corrupt political system which is undermining American democracy and it's important we talk about that and understand that. As a result of the disastrous Citizens United Supreme Court decision, corporations and billionaires are able to spend unlimited sums of money on elections. The result is that today a handful of billionaires are spending hundreds of millions of dollars every single year, often on ugly 30-second TV adds, helping to elect candidates who represent the rich and the powerful get elected.

And we are seeing the results of how oligarchy functions right now in Congress where the Republican leadership wants to throw 23 million American off of health insurance, cut Medicaid by over $800 billion, defund Planned Parenthood, cut food stamps and other nutrition programs by over $200 billion, cut Head Start and after school programs, and by the way, make drastic cuts in Pell grants and other programs that help working class kids be able to go to college.

And, unbelievably, at exactly the same time that they are throwing people off health care, making it

harder to people to go to college, they have the
chutzpah to provide the $300 billion in tax breaks to
the top 1%. In other words, the very, very rich are
getting richer and they get huge tax cuts. The working
class and the middle class are struggling and they are
seeing drastic cuts in life or death programs that could
mean survival or not for those families.

Now, in response to these very serious crises it
seems to me that we have two choices. First we can
throw up our hands in despair. We can say, "I am not
going to get involved." That is understandable. But it
is wrong.

Because the issues that we deal with today — the
economic issues, the social issues, the racial issues, the
environmental issues — not only impact your lives,
they impact the lives of future generations and you do
not have the moral right to turn your back on saving
this planet and saving future generations.

The truth is that the only rational choice we
have, the only real response we can make is to stand
up and fight back — reclaim American democracy
and create a government that works for all of us, not
just the 1%.

And for us to do that it is necessary that we fight
for a vision of a new America. An America based on
progressive, humane values, not the values of the
oligarchy.

And what does that mean, briefly in concrete terms?

It means that, no, we are not going to throw 23 million Americans off the health care they have. We are going to bring about health care for all as a right, not a privilege.

It means that, no, we are not, as the current administration does, deny the reality of climate change. We are going to take on the fossil fuel industry, transform our energy system away from fossil fuels to energy efficiency and sustainable energy.

It means no we are not going to cut Pell grants and other student assistance. We are going to do what Germany, what Scandinavia, what countries all over the world do. And that is to make certain the public colleges and universities are tuition-free and we're going to significantly lower student debt because we believe that anyone in America who has the ability and the desire to be able to get a higher education regardless of his or her income.

And no we're not going to do what the attorney general of the United States now wants. We're not going to put more people in jail. We're going to fix a broken criminal justice system and invest in education and jobs for our young people, not more jails and incarceration.

No, we're not going to defund Planned Parenthood. We're going to vigorously defend a woman's right to choose.

My friends, let me conclude by saying this. We live in the wealthiest country in the history of the world. We are seeing exploding technology, which if used well, has extraordinary potential to improve life. We are an intelligent and hardworking people. If we are prepared to stand together; if we take on greed and selfishness; if we refuse to allow demagogues to divide us up there is no end to what the great people of our nation can accomplish.

So today as you graduate Brooklyn College, my message to you is very simple. Think big, not small, and help us create the nation that we all know we can become. Thank you all very much.

CHAPTER 3
The Political Revolution...

June 16, 2016

Election days come and go. But political and social revolutions that attempt to transform our society never end. They continue every day, every week and every month in the fight to create a nation of social and economic justice. That's what the trade union movement is about. That's what the civil rights movement is about. That's what the women's movement is about. That's what the gay rights movement is about. That's what the environmental movement is about.

And that's what this campaign has been about over the past year. That's what the political revolution is about and that's why the political revolution must continue into the future.

Real change never takes place from the top down, or in the living rooms of wealthy campaign contributors. It always occurs from the bottom on up – when tens of millions of people say "enough is enough" and become engaged in the fight for justice. That's what the political revolution we helped start is all about. That's why the political revolution must continue.

When we began this campaign a little over a year ago, we had no political organization, no money and very little name recognition. The media determined that we were a fringe campaign. Nobody thought we were going anywhere.

Well, a lot has changed over a year.

During this campaign, we won more than 12 million votes. We won 22 state primaries and caucuses. We came very close – within 2 points or less – in five more states.

In other words, our vision for the future of this country is not some kind of fringe idea. It is not a radical idea. It is mainstream. It is what millions of Americans believe in and want to see happen.

And something else extraordinarily important happened in this campaign that makes me very optimistic about the future of our country – something that, frankly, I had not anticipated. In virtually every state that we contested we won the overwhelming majority of the votes of people 45 years of age or younger, sometimes, may I say, by huge numbers. These are the people who are determined to shape the future of this country. These are the people who ARE the future of this country.

Together, in this campaign, 1.5 million people came out to our rallies and town meetings in almost every state in the country.

Together, hundreds of thousands of volunteers made 75 million phone calls urging their fellow citizens into action.

Together, our canvassers knocked on more than 5 million doors.

Together, we hosted 74,000 meetings in every state and territory in this country.

Together, 2.7 million people made over 8 million individual contributions to our campaign – more contributions at this point than any campaign in American history. Amazingly, the bulk of those contributions came from low-income and working people whose donations averaged $27 apiece. In an unprecedented way, we showed the world that we could run a strong national campaign without being dependent on the big-money interests whose greed has done so much to damage our country.

And let me give a special thanks to the financial support we received from students struggling to repay their college loans, from seniors and disabled vets on Social Security, from workers earning starvation wages and even from people who were unemployed.

In every single state that we contested we took on virtually the entire political establishment – U.S.

senators, members of Congress, governors, mayors, state legislators and local party leaders. To those relatively few elected officials who had the courage to stand with us, I say thank you. We must continue working together into the future.

This campaign has never been about any single candidate. It is always about transforming America.

It is about ending a campaign finance system which is corrupt and allows billionaires to buy elections.

It is about ending the grotesque level of wealth and income inequality that we are experiencing where almost all new wealth and income goes to the people on top, where the 20 wealthiest people own more wealth than the bottom 150 million.

It is about creating an economy that works for all of us, not just the 1 percent.

It is about ending the disgrace of native Americans who live on the Pine Ridge, South Dakota, reservation having a life expectancy lower than many third-world countries.

It is about ending the incredible despair that exists in many parts of this country where – as a result of unemployment and low wages, suicide, drugs and alcohol – millions of Americans are now dying, in an a historical way, at a younger age than their parents.

It is about ending the disgrace of having the highest level of childhood poverty of almost any major country on earth and having public school systems in inner cities that are totally failing our children – where kids now stand a greater chance of ending up in jail than ending up with a college degree.

It is about ending the disgrace that millions of undocumented people in this country continue to live in fear and are exploited every day on their jobs because they have no legal rights.

It is about ending the disgrace of tens of thousands of Americans dying every year from preventable deaths because they either lack health insurance, have high deductibles or cannot afford the outrageously high cost of the prescription drugs they need.

It is about ending the disgrace of hundreds of thousands of bright young people unable to go to college because their families are poor or working class, while millions more struggle with suffocating levels of student debt.

It is about ending the pain of a young single mother in Nevada, in tears, telling me that she doesn't know how she and her daughter can make it on $10.45 an hour. And the reality that today millions of our fellow Americans are working at starvation wages.

It is about ending the disgrace of a mother in Flint, Michigan, telling me what has happened to the intellectual development of her child as a result of lead in the water in that city, of many thousands of homes in California and other communities unable to drink the polluted water that comes out of their faucets.

In America. In the year 2016. In a nation whose infrastructure is crumbling before our eyes.

It is about ending the disgrace that too many veterans still sleep out on the streets, that homelessness is increasing and that tens of millions of Americans, because of a lack of affordable housing, are paying 40, 50 percent or more of their limited incomes to put a roof over their heads.

It is about ending the disgrace that, in a given year, corporations making billions in profit avoid paying a nickel in taxes because they stash their money in the Cayman Islands and other tax havens.

This campaign is about defeating Donald Trump, the Republican candidate for president. After centuries of racism, sexism and discrimination of all forms in our country we do not need a major party candidate who makes bigotry the cornerstone of his campaign. We cannot have a president who insults

Mexicans and Latinos, Muslims, women and African-Americans. We cannot have a president who, in the midst of so much income and wealth inequality, wants to give hundreds of billions of dollars in tax breaks to the very rich. We cannot have a president who, despite all of the scientific evidence, believes that climate change is a hoax.

The major political task that we face in the next five months is to make certain that Donald Trump is defeated and defeated badly. And I personally intend to begin my role in that process in a very short period of time.

But defeating Donald Trump cannot be our only goal. We must continue our grassroots efforts to create the America that we know we can become. And we must take that energy into the Democratic National Convention on July 25 in Philadelphia where we will have more than 1,900 delegates.

I recently had the opportunity to meet with Secretary Clinton and discuss some of the very important issues facing our country and the Democratic Party. It is no secret that Secretary Clinton and I have strong disagreements on some very important issues. It is also true that our views are quite close on others. I look forward, in the coming weeks, to continued discussions between the two campaigns to make certain that your voices are heard and that the Democratic Party passes the most progressive platform in its history and that Democrats actually fight for that agenda. I also look forward to working with Secretary Clinton to transform the Democratic Party so that it becomes a party of working people and young people, and not just wealthy campaign contributors: a party that has the courage to take on Wall Street, the pharmaceutical industry, the fossil fuel industry and the other powerful special interests that dominate our political and economic life.

As I have said throughout this campaign, the Democratic Party must support raising the federal minimum wage to $15 an hour, and create millions of jobs rebuilding our crumbling infrastructure.

We must ensure that women will no longer make 79-cents on the dollar compared to men and that we fight for pay equity.

We must fight to make certain that women throughout the country have the right to control their own bodies.

We must protect the right of our gay brothers and sisters to marriage equality in every state America.

As the recent tragedy in Orlando has made crystal clear, we must ban the sale and distribution of assault weapons, end the gun show loophole and expand instant background checks.

We must defeat the Trans-Pacific Partnership and make certain that that bad trade deal does not get a vote in a lame-duck session of Congress.

We must resist all efforts to cut Social Security and, in fact, expand benefits for our seniors and disabled veterans.

We must understand that the greed, recklessness and illegal behavior on Wall Street has to end, that we need to pass modern-day Glass-Steagall legislation and that we need to break up the biggest financial institutions in this country who not only remain too big to fail but who prevent the kind of vigorous competition that a healthy financial system requires.

We must aggressively combat climate change and transform our energy system, move to energy efficiency and sustainable energy and impose a tax on carbon. It means that, in order to protect our water supply, we ban fracking.

We must compete effectively in a global economy by making public colleges and universities tuition free and substantially reduce student debt.

We must join the rest of the industrialized world and guarantee health care to all people as a right and not a privilege.

We must end the disgrace of having more people in jail than any other country on earth and move toward real criminal justice reform at the federal, state and local levels.

We must pass comprehensive immigration reform and provide a path toward citizenship for 11 million undocumented people.

We must take a hard look at the waste, cost overruns and inefficiencies in every branch of government –including the Department of Defense. And we must make certain our brave young men and women in the military are not thrown into perpetual warfare in the Middle East or other wars we should not be fighting.

But the political revolution means much more than fighting for our ideals at the Democratic National Convention and defeating Donald Trump.

It means that, at every level, we continue the fight to make our society a nation of economic, social, racial and environmental justice.

It means that we can no longer ignore the fact that, sadly, the current Democratic Party leadership has turned its back on dozens of states in this country and has allowed right-wing politicians to win elections in some states with virtually no opposition – including some of the poorest states in America. The

Democratic Party needs a 50-state strategy. We may not win in every state tomorrow but we will never win unless we recruit good candidates and develop organizations that can compete effectively in the future. We must provide resources to those states which have so long been ignored.

Most importantly, the Democratic Party needs leadership which is prepared to open its doors and welcome into its ranks working people and young people. That is the energy that we need to transform the Democratic Party, take on the special interests and transform our country.

Here is a cold, hard fact that must be addressed. Since 2009, some 900 legislative seats have been lost to Republicans in state after state throughout this country. In fact, the Republican Party now controls 31 state legislatures and controls both the governors' mansions and statehouses in 23 states. That is unacceptable.

We need to start engaging at the local and state level in an unprecedented way. Hundreds of thousands of volunteers helped us make political history during the last year. These are people deeply concerned about the future of our country and their own communities. Now we need many of them to start running for school boards, city councils, county commissions, state legislatures and governorships.

State and local governments make enormously important decisions and we cannot allow right-wing Republicans to increasingly control them.

I hope very much that many of you listening tonight are prepared to engage at that level. Please go to my website at berniesanders.com/win to learn more about how you can effectively run for office or get involved in politics at the local or state level. I have no doubt that with the energy and enthusiasm our campaign has shown that we can win significant numbers of local and state elections if people are prepared to become involved. I also hope people will give serious thought to running for statewide offices and the U.S. Congress.

And when we talk about transforming America, it is not just about elections. Many of my Republican colleagues believe that government is the enemy, that we need to eviscerate and privatize virtually all aspects of government – whether it is Social Security, Medicare, the VA, EPA, the Postal Service or public education. I strongly disagree. In a democratic civilized society, government must play an enormously important role in protecting all of us and our planet. But in order for government to work efficiently and effectively, we need to attract great and dedicated people from all walks of life. We need people who are dedicated to public service and can provide the services we need in a high quality and efficient way.

When we talk about a Medicare-for-all health care program and the need to make sure all of our people have quality health care, it means that we need tens of thousands of new doctors, nurses, dentists, psychologists and other medical personnel who are prepared to practice in areas where people today lack access to that care.

It means that we need hundreds of thousands of people to become childcare workers and teachers so that our young people will get the best education available in the world.

It means that as we combat climate change and transform our energy system away from fossil fuels, we need scientists and engineers and entrepreneurs who will help us make energy efficiency, solar energy, wind energy, geothermal and other developing technologies as efficient and cost effective as possible.

It means that as we rebuild our crumbling infrastructure, we need millions of skilled construction workers of all kinds.

It means that when we talk about growing our economy and creating jobs, we need great business people who can produce and distribute the products and services we need in a way that respects their employees and the environment.

In other words, we need a new generation of people actively involved in public service who are prepared to provide the quality of life the American people deserve.

Let me conclude by once again thanking everyone who has helped in this campaign in one way or another. We have begun the long and arduous process of transforming America, a fight that will continue tomorrow, next week, next year and into the future.

My hope is that when future historians look back and describe how our country moved forward into reversing the drift toward oligarchy, and created a government which represents all the people and not just the few, they will note that, to a significant degree, that effort began with the political revolution of 2016.

Thank you very much. Good night.

CHAPTER 4
The Urgency of a Moral Economy
April 15, 2016

I am honored to be with you today and was pleased to receive your invitation to speak to this conference of The Pontifical Academy of Social Sciences. Today we celebrate the encyclical Centesimus Annus and reflect on its meaning for our world a quarter-century after it was presented by Pope John Paul II. With the fall of Communism, Pope John Paul II gave a clarion call for human freedom in its truest sense: freedom that defends the dignity of every person and that is always oriented towards the common good.

The Church's social teachings, stretching back to the first modern encyclical about the industrial economy, Rerum Novarum in 1891, to Centesimus Annus, to Pope Francis's inspiring encyclical Laudato Si' this past year, have grappled with the challenges of the market economy. There are few places in modern thought that rival the depth and insight of the Church's moral teachings on the market economy.

Over a century ago, Pope Leo XIII highlighted economic issues and challenges in Rerum Novarum that continue to haunt us today, such as what he called "the enormous wealth of a few as opposed to the poverty of the many."

And let us be clear. That situation is worse today. In the year 2016, the top one percent of the people on this planet own more wealth than the bottom 99 percent, while the wealthiest 60 people – 60 people – own more than the bottom half – 3 1/2 billion people. At a time when so few have so much, and so many have so little, we must reject the foundations of this contemporary economy as immoral and unsustainable.

The words of Centesimus Annus likewise resonate with us today. One striking example:

Furthermore, society and the State must ensure wage levels adequate for the maintenance of the worker and his family, including a certain amount for savings. This requires a continuous effort to improve workers' training and capability so that their work will be more skilled and productive, as well as careful controls and adequate legislative measures to block shameful forms of exploitation, especially to the disadvantage of the most vulnerable workers, of immigrants and of those on the margins of society. The role of trade unions in negotiating minimum salaries and working conditions is decisive in this area. (Para15)

The essential wisdom of Centesimus Annus is this: A market economy is beneficial for productivity and economic freedom. But if we let the quest for profits dominate society; if workers become disposable cogs of the financial system; if vast inequalities of power and wealth lead to marginalization of the poor and the powerless; then the common good is squandered and the market economy fails us. Pope John Paul II puts it this way: profit that is the result of "illicit exploitation, speculation, or the breaking of solidarity among working people . . . has not justification, and represents an abuse in the sight of God and man." (Para43).

We are now twenty-five years after the fall of Communist rule in Eastern Europe. Yet we have to acknowledge that Pope John Paul's warnings about the excesses of untrammeled finance were deeply prescient. Twenty-five years after Centesimus Annus, speculation, illicit financial flows, environmental destruction, and the weakening of the rights of workers is far more severe than it was a quarter century ago. Financial excesses, indeed widespread financial criminality on Wall Street, played a direct role in causing the world's worst financial crisis since the Great Depression.

We need a political analysis as well as a moral and anthropological analysis to understand what has happened since 1991. We can say that with unregulated globalization, a world market economy

built on speculative finance burst through the legal,
political, and moral constraints that had once served
to protect the common good. In my country, home of
the world's largest financial markets, globalization was
used as a pretext to deregulate the banks, ending
decades of legal protections for working people and
small businesses. Politicians joined hands with the
leading bankers to allow the banks to become "too
big to fail." The result: eight years ago the American
economy and much of the world was plunged into the
worst economic decline since the 1930s. Working
people lost their jobs, their homes and their savings,
while the government bailed out the banks.

Inexplicably, the United States political system
doubled down on this reckless financial deregulation,
when the U.S. Supreme Court in a series of deeply
misguided decisions, unleashed an unprecedented
flow of money into American politics. These
decisions culminated in the infamous Citizen United
case, which opened the financial spigots for huge
campaign donations by billionaires and large
corporations to turn the U.S. political system to their
narrow and greedy advantage. It has established a
system in which billionaires can buy elections. Rather
than an economy aimed at the common good, we
have been left with an economy operated for the top
1 percent, who get richer and richer as the working
class, the young and the poor fall further and further
behind. And the billionaires and banks have reaped

the returns of their campaign investments, in the form of special tax privileges, imbalanced trade agreements that favor investors over workers, and that even give multinational companies extra-judicial power over governments that are trying to regulate them.

But as both Pope John Paul II and Pope Francis have warned us and the world, the consequences have been even direr than the disastrous effects of financial bubbles and falling living standards of working-class families. Our very soul as a nation has suffered as the public lost faith in political and social institutions. As Pope Francis has stated: "Man is not in charge today, money is in charge, money rules." And the Pope has also stated: "We have created new idols. The worship of the golden calf of old has found a new and heartless image in the cult of money and the dictatorship of an economy which is faceless and lacking any truly humane goal."

And further: "While the income of a minority is increasing exponentially, that of the majority is crumbling. This imbalance results from ideologies which uphold the absolute autonomy of markets and financial speculation, and thus deny the right of control to States, which are themselves charged with providing for the common good."

Pope Francis has called on the world to say: "No

to a financial system that rules rather than serves" in Evangeli Gaudium. And he called upon financial executives and political leaders to pursue financial reform that is informed by ethical considerations. He stated plainly and powerfully that the role of wealth and resources in a moral economy must be that of servant, not master.

The widening gaps between the rich and poor, the desperation of the marginalized, the power of corporations over politics, is not a phenomenon of the United States alone. The excesses of the unregulated global economy have caused even more damage in the developing countries. They suffer not only from the boom-bust cycles on Wall Street, but from a world economy that puts profits over pollution, oil companies over climate safety, and arms trade over peace. And as an increasing share of new wealth and income goes to a small fraction of those at the top, fixing this gross inequality has become a central challenge. The issue of wealth and income inequality is the great economic issue of our time, the great political issue of our time, and the great moral issue of our time. It is an issue that we must confront in my nation and across the world.

Pope Francis has given the most powerful name to the predicament of modern society: the Globalization of Indifference. "Almost without being aware of it," he noted, "we end up being incapable of feeling compassion at the outcry of the poor, weeping for other people's pain, and feeling a need to help them, as though all this were someone else's responsibility and not our own." We have seen on Wall Street that financial fraud became not only the norm but in many ways the new business model. Top bankers have shown no shame for their bad behavior and have made no apologies to the public. The billions and billions of dollars of fines they have paid for financial fraud are just another cost of doing business, another short cut to unjust profits.

Some might feel that it is hopeless to fight the economic juggernaut, that once the market economy escaped the boundaries of morality it would be impossible to bring the economy back under the dictates of morality and the common good. I am told time and time again by the rich and powerful, and the mainstream media that represent them, that we should be "practical," that we should accept the status quo; that a truly moral economy is beyond our reach. Yet Pope Francis himself is surely the world's greatest demonstration against such a surrender to despair and cynicism. He has opened the eyes of the world once again to the claims of mercy, justice and the possibilities of a better world. He is inspiring the world to find a new global consensus for our common home.

I see that hope and sense of possibility every day

among America's young people. Our youth are no longer satisfied with corrupt and broken politics and an economy of stark inequality and injustice. They are not satisfied with the destruction of our environment by a fossil fuel industry whose greed has put short term profits ahead of climate change and the future of our planet. They want to live in harmony with nature, not destroy it. They are calling out for a return to fairness; for an economy that defends the common good by ensuring that every person, rich or poor, has access to quality health care, nutrition and education.

As Pope Francis made powerfully clear last year in Laudato Si', we have the technology and know-how to solve our problems – from poverty to climate change to health care to protection of biodiversity. We also have the vast wealth to do so, especially if the rich pay their way in fair taxes rather than hiding their funds in the world's tax and secrecy havens- as the Panama Papers have shown.

The challenges facing our planet are not mainly technological or even financial, because as a world we are rich enough to increase our investments in skills, infrastructure, and technological know-how to meet our needs and to protect the planet. Our challenge is mostly a moral one, to redirect our efforts and vision to the common good. Centesimus Annus, which we celebrate and reflect on today, and Laudato Si', are powerful, eloquent and hopeful messages of this possibility. It is up to us to learn from them, and to move boldly toward the common good in our time.

CHAPTER 5
Wall Street & the Economy

January 5, 2016

The American people are catching on. They understand that something is profoundly wrong when, in our country today, the top one-tenth of 1 percent own almost as much wealth as the bottom 90 percent and when the 20 richest people own more wealth than the bottom 150 million Americans – half of our population. They know that the system is rigged when the average person is working longer hours for lower wages, while 58 percent of all new income goes to the top 1 percent.

They also know that a handful of people on Wall Street have extraordinary power over the economic and political life of our country. As most people know, in the 1990s and later, the financial interests spent billions of dollars in lobbying and campaign contributions to force through Congress the deregulation of Wall Street, the repeal of the Glass-Steagall Act and the weakening of consumer protection laws in states.

They spent this money in order to get the government off their backs and to show the American people what they could do with that new-won freedom. Well, they sure showed the American people. In 2008, the greed, recklessness and illegal behavior on Wall Street nearly destroyed the U.S. and global economy.

Millions of Americans lost their jobs, their homes and their life savings.

While Wall Street received the largest taxpayer bailout in the history of the world with no strings attached, the American middle class continues to disappear, poverty is increasing and the gap between the very rich and everyone else is growing wider and wider. And Wall Street executives still receive huge compensation packages as if the financial crisis they created never happened.

Greed, fraud, dishonesty and arrogance, these are the words that best describe the reality of Wall Street today.

So, to those on Wall Street who may be listening today, let me be very clear. Greed is not good. In fact, the greed of Wall Street and corporate America is destroying the fabric of our nation. And, here is a New Year's Resolution that I will keep if elected president. If you do not end your greed, we will end it for you.

We will no longer tolerate an economy and a political system that has been rigged by Wall Street to benefit the wealthiest Americans in this country at the expense of everyone else.

While President Obama deserves credit for improving this economy after the Wall Street crash, the reality is that a lot of unfinished business remains to be done.

Our goal must be to create a financial system and an economy that works for all Americans, not just a handful of billionaires.

That means we have got to end, once and for all, the scheme that is nothing more than a free insurance policy for Wall Street, the policy of "too big to fail."

We need a banking system that is part of the productive economy – making loans at affordable rates to small- and medium-sized businesses so that we create decent-paying jobs. Wall Street cannot continue to be an island unto itself, gambling trillions in risky financial instruments, making huge profits and assured that, if their schemes fail, the taxpayers will be there to bail them out.

In 2008, the taxpayers of this country bailed out Wall Street because we were told they were "too big to fail." Yet, today, 3 out of the 4 largest financial institutions (JP Morgan Chase, Bank of America and Wells Fargo) are nearly 80 percent bigger than before we bailed them out. Incredibly, the six largest banks in this country issue more than two-thirds of all credit cards and more than 35 percent of all mortgages. They control more than 95 percent of all financial derivatives and hold more than 40 percent of all bank deposits. Their assets are equivalent to nearly 60 percent of our GDP. Enough is enough.

If a bank is too big to fail, it is too big to exist. When it comes to Wall Street reform that must be our bottom line. This is true not just from a risk perspective and the fear of another bailout. It is also true from the reality that a handful of huge financial institutions simply have too much economic and political power over this country.

If Teddy Roosevelt, the Republican trust-buster, were alive today, he would say "break 'em up." And he would be right.

And, here's how I will accomplish that.

Within the first 100 days of my administration, I will require the secretary of the Treasury Department to establish a "Too-Big-to Fail" list of commercial banks, shadow banks and insurance companies whose failure would pose a catastrophic risk to the United States economy without a taxpayer bailout.

Within one year, my administration will break these institutions up so that they no longer pose a grave threat to the economy as authorized under Section 121 of the Dodd-Frank Act.

And, I will fight to reinstate a 21st Century Glass-Steagall Act to clearly separate commercial banking, investment banking and insurance services. Let's be clear: this legislation, introduced by my colleague Senator Elizabeth Warren, aims at the heart of the shadow banking system.

In my view, Senator Warren, is right. Dodd-Frank should have broken up Citigroup and other "too- big-to-fail" banks into pieces. And that's exactly what we need to do. And that's what I commit to do as president.

Now, my opponent, Secretary Clinton says that Glass-Steagall would not have prevented the financial crisis because shadow banks like AIG and Lehman Brothers, not big commercial banks, were the real culprits.

Secretary Clinton is wrong.

Shadow banks did gamble recklessly, but where did that money come from? It came from the federally-insured bank deposits of big commercial banks – something that would have been banned under the Glass-Steagall Act.

Let's not forget: President Franklin Roosevelt signed this bill into law precisely to prevent Wall Street speculators from causing another Great Depression. And, it worked for more than five

decades until Wall Street watered it down under
President Reagan and killed it under President
Clinton.

And, let's not kid ourselves. The Federal Reserve
and the Treasury Department didn't just bail out
shadow banks. As a result of an amendment that I
offered to audit the emergency lending activities of
the Federal Reserve during the financial crisis, we
learned that the Fed provided more than $16 trillion
in short-term, low-interest loans to every major
financial institution in the country including
Citigroup, JP Morgan Chase, Bank of America, Wells
Fargo, not to mention large corporations, foreign
banks, and foreign central banks throughout the
world.

Secretary Clinton says we just need to impose a
few more fees and regulations on the financial
industry. I disagree.

As former Secretary of Labor Robert Reich has
said and I quote: "Giant Wall Street banks continue
to threaten the wellbeing of millions of Americans,
but what to do? Bernie Sanders says break them up
and resurrect the Glass-Steagall Act that once
separated investment from commercial banking.
Hillary Clinton says charge them a bit more and
oversee them more carefully … Hillary Clinton's
proposals would only invite more dilution and finagle.

The only way to contain the Street's excesses is with reforms so big, bold, and public they can't be watered down – busting up the biggest banks and resurrecting Glass-Steagall."

Secretary Reich is right. Real Wall Street reform means breaking up the big banks and re-establishing firewalls that separates risk taking from traditional banking.

My opponent says that, as a senator, she told bankers to "cut it out" and end their destructive behavior. But, in my view, establishment politicians are the ones who need to "cut it out." The reality is that Congress doesn't regulate Wall Street. Wall Street, its lobbyists and their billions of dollars regulate Congress. We must change that reality, and as president I will.

It is no secret that millions of Americans have become disillusioned with our political process. They don't vote. They don't believe much of what comes out of Washington. They don't think anyone is there representing their interests. In my view, one of the reasons for that deep disillusionment is the widespread understanding that our criminal justice system is broken and grossly unfair – and that we do not have equal justice under the law. The average American sees kids being arrested and sometimes even jailed for possessing marijuana or other minor crimes. But when it comes to Wall Street executives, some of the wealthiest and most powerful people in this country, whose illegal behavior caused pain and suffering for millions – somehow nothing happens to them. No police record. No jail time. No justice.

We live in a country today that has an economy that is rigged, a campaign finance system which is corrupt and a criminal justice system which, too often, does not dispense justice.

Not one major Wall Street executive has been prosecuted for causing the near collapse of our entire economy.

That will change under my administration. "Equal Justice Under Law" will not just be words engraved on the entrance of the Supreme Court. It will be the standard that applies to Wall Street and all Americans.

It seems like almost every few weeks we read about one giant financial institution after another being fined or reaching settlements for their reckless, unfair and deceptive activities.

Some people believe that this is an aberration: that we have an honest financial system in which, every now and then, major financial institutions do something wrong and get caught. In my view, the evidence suggests that would be an incorrect analysis.

The reality is that fraud is the business model on Wall Street. It is not the exception to the rule. It is the rule. And in a weak regulatory climate the likelihood is that Wall Street gets away with a lot more illegal behavior than we know of.

How many times have we heard the myth that what Wall Street did may have been wrong but it wasn't illegal?

Let me help shatter that myth today.

Since 2009, major financial institutions in this country have been fined $204 billion. $204 billion. And that takes place in a weak regulatory climate.

Here are just a few examples of when major banks were caught doing illegal activity.

In August 2014, Bank of America settled a case with the Department of Justice for more than $16 billion on charges that the bank misled investors about the riskiness of mortgage-backed securities it sold in the run-up to the crisis.

In November of 2013, JP Morgan settled a case for $13 billion with the Department of Justice and the Federal Housing Finance Agency over charges the bank knowingly sold securities made up of low-quality mortgages to Fannie Mae and Freddie Mac.

In June of 2014, BNP Paribas was sentenced to

five years' probation and was ordered to pay $8.9 billion in penalties by a U.S. District Judge in Manhattan after this bank pled guilty to charges of violating sanctions by conducting business in Sudan, Iran and Cuba.

Let me read you a few headlines and you tell me how it makes sense that not one executive was prosecuted for fraud.

CNN Headline, May 20, 2015: "5 big banks pay $5.4 billion for rigging currencies." Those banks include JPMorgan Chase and Citigroup.

Headline from the International Business Times (February 24, 2015): "Big Banks Under Investigation For Allegedly Fixing Precious Metals Prices." The Banks under investigation included Goldman Sachs and JPMorgan Chase.

Headline from The Real News Network (November 26, 2013): "Documents in JPMorgan settlement reveal how every large bank in the U.S. has committed mortgage fraud."

Headline from The Washington Post (March 14, 2014): "In lawsuit, FDIC accuses 16 big banks of fraud, conspiracy," which included Bank of America, Citigroup and JP Morgan Chase.

Headline from the Guardian (April 2, 2011):

"How a big U.S. bank laundered billions from Mexico's murderous drug gangs." This article talks about how Wachovia (which was acquired by Wells Fargo) aided Mexican drug cartels in transferring billions of dollars in illegal drug money. Here is what the federal prosecutor (Jeffrey Sloman) said about this: "Wachovia's blatant disregard for our banking laws gave international cocaine cartels a virtual carte blanche to finance their operations."

Yet, the total fine for this offense was less than 2% of the bank's $12.3 billion profit for 2009 and no one went to jail. No one went to jail.

And, if that's not bad enough, here's another one.

Headline: The Wall Street Journal, February 9, 2011: "J.P. Morgan Apologizes for Military Foreclosures." Here is a case where JP Morgan Chase, the largest bank in America, wrecked the finances of 4,000 military families in violation of the Civil Service Members Relief Act, yet no one went to jail.

And, when I say that the business model of Wall Street is fraud that is not just Bernie Sanders talking. That is what financial executives told the University of Notre Dame in a study on the ethics of the financial services industry last year.

According to this study, 51 percent of Wall Street

executives making more than $500,000 a year found it likely that their competitors have engaged in unethical or illegal activity in order to gain an edge in the market.

More than one-third of financial executives have either witnessed or have firsthand knowledge of wrongdoing in the workplace.

Nearly one in five financial service professionals believe they must engage in illegal or unethical activity to be successful.

Twenty-five percent of financial executives have signed or been asked to sign a confidentiality agreement that would prohibit reporting illegal or unethical activities to the authorities.

Here's what one banker from Barclays said in 2010, when he was caught trying to price-fix the $5 trillion-per-day currency market: "If you ain't cheating, you ain't trying."

Here's what an analyst from Standard & Poors said in 2008, "Let's hope we are all wealthy and retired by the time this house of cards falters."

This country can no longer afford to tolerate the culture of fraud and corruption on Wall Street.

Under my administration, Wall Street CEOs will no longer receive a get-out-of jail free card. Big banks

will not be too big to fail. Big bankers will not be too
big to jail.

As president, I will nominate and appoint people
with a track record of standing up to power, rather
than those who have made millions defending Wall
Street CEOs. Goldman Sachs and other Wall Street
banks will not be represented in my administration.

And, if we are serious about reforming our
financial system, we have got to establish a tax on
Wall Street speculators. We have got to discourage
reckless gambling on Wall Street and encourage
productive investments in the job-creating economy.

We will use the revenue from this tax to make
public colleges and universities tuition free. During
the financial crisis, the middle class of this country
bailed out Wall Street. Now, it's Wall Street's turn to
help the middle class.

We cannot have a safe and sound financial
system if we cannot trust the credit agencies to
accurately rate financial products. And, the only way
we can restore that trust is to make sure credit rating
agencies cannot make a profit from Wall Street.

Investors would not have bought the risky
mortgage backed derivatives that led to the Great
Recession if credit agencies did not give these
worthless financial products triple-A ratings – ratings

that they knew were bogus.

And, the reason these risky financial schemes were given such favorable ratings is simple. Wall Street paid for them.

Under my administration, we will turn for-profit credit rating agencies into non-profit institutions, independent from Wall Street. No longer will Wall Street be able to pick and choose which credit agency will rate their products.

If we are going to create a financial system that works for all Americans, we have got to stop financial institutions from ripping off the American people by charging sky-high interest rates and outrageous fees.

In my view, it is unacceptable that Americans are paying a $4 or $5 fee each time they go to the ATM.

It is unacceptable that millions of Americans are paying credit card interest rates of 20 or 30 percent.

The Bible has a term for this practice. It's called usury. And in The Divine Comedy, Dante reserved a special place in the Seventh Circle of Hell for those who charged people usurious interest rates.

Today, we don't need the hellfire and the pitch forks, we don't need the rivers of boiling blood, but we do need a national usury law.

Today, we need to cap interest rates on credit cards and consumer loans at 15 percent.

In 1980, Congress passed legislation to require credit unions to cap interest rates on their loans at no more than 15 percent. And, that law has worked well. Unlike big banks, credit unions did not receive a huge bailout from the taxpayers of this country. It is time to extend this cap to every lender in America.

We must also cap ATM fees at $2.00. People should not have to pay a 10 percent fee for withdrawing $40 of their own money out of an ATM.

Big banks need to stop acting like loan sharks and start acting like responsible lenders.

We also need to give Americans affordable banking options.

The reality is that, unbelievably, millions of low-income Americans live in communities where there are no normal banking services. Today, if you live in a low-income community and you need to cash a check or get a loan to pay for a car repair or a medical emergency, where do you go?

You go to a payday lender who could charge an interest rate of over 300 percent and trap you into a vicious cycle of debt. That is unacceptable.

We need to stop payday lenders from ripping off

millions of Americans. Post offices exist in almost every community in our country. One important way to provide decent banking opportunities for low income communities is to allow the U.S. postal Service to engage in basic banking services, and that's what I will fight for.

Further, we need to structurally reform the Federal Reserve to make it a more democratic institution responsive to the needs of ordinary Americans, not just the billionaires on Wall Street.

When Wall Street was on the verge of collapse, the Federal Reserve acted with a fierce sense of urgency to save the financial system. We need the Fed to act with the same boldness to combat unemployment and low wages.

In my view, it is unacceptable that the Federal Reserve has been hijacked by the very bankers it is in charge of regulating. I think the American people would be shocked to learn that Jamie Dimon, the CEO of JP Morgan Chase, served on the board of the New York Fed at the same time that his bank received a $391 billion bailout from the Federal Reserve. That is a clear conflict of interest that I would ban as president. When I am elected, the foxes will no longer be guarding the henhouse at the Fed. Under my administration, banking industry executives will no longer be allowed to serve on the Fed's boards and handpick its members and staff.

Further, the Fed should stop paying financial institutions interest to keep money out of the economy and parked at the Fed. Incredibly, the excess reserves of financial institutions that are sitting in the Federal Reserve has grown from less than $2 billion in 2008 to $2.4 trillion today. That is absurd.

Instead of paying banks interest on these reserves, the Fed should charge them a fee that could be used to provide affordable loans to small businesses to create hundreds of thousands of jobs.

Finally, let me tell you what no other candidate will tell you. No president, not Bernie Sanders or anyone else, can effectively address the economic crises facing the working families of this country alone. The truth is that Wall Street, corporate America, the corporate media and wealthy campaign donors are just too powerful.

What this campaign is about is building a political movement which revitalizes American democracy, which brings millions of people together – black and white, Latino, Asian-American, Native American – young and old, men and women, gay and straight, native born and immigrant, people of all religions.

Yes. Wall Street has enormous economic and political power. Yes. Wall Street makes huge campaign contributions, they have thousands of lobbyists and they provide very generous speaking fees to those who go before them.

Yes. They have an endless supply of money. But we have something they don't have. And that is that when millions of working families stand together, demanding fundamental changes in our financial system, we have the power to bring about that change.

Yes, we can make our economy work for all Americans, not just a handful of wealthy speculators. And, now more than ever, that is exactly what we must do.

And so my message to you today is straightforward: If elected president, I will rein in Wall Street so they can't crash our economy again.

Will they like me? No. Will they begin to play by the rules if I'm president? You better believe it.

Thank you and I look forward to working with the most powerful force in our great nation, not the Barons of Wall Street but the people our government was created to serve.

CHAPTER 6
Democratic Socialism in the U.S.A

November 19, 2015

In his inaugural remarks in January 1937, in the midst of the Great Depression, President Franklin Delano Roosevelt looked out at the nation and this is what he saw.

He saw tens of millions of its citizens denied the basic necessities of life.

He saw millions of families trying to live on incomes so meager that the pall of family disaster hung over them day by day.

He saw millions denied education, recreation, and the opportunity to better their lot and the lot of their children.

He saw millions lacking the means to buy the products they needed and by their poverty and lack of disposable income denying employment to many other millions.

He saw one-third of a nation ill-housed, ill-clad, ill-nourished.

And he acted. Against the ferocious opposition of the ruling class of his day, people he called economic royalists, Roosevelt implemented a series of programs that put millions of people back to work, took them out of poverty and restored their faith in government. He redefined the relationship of the federal government to the people of our country. He combated cynicism, fear and despair. He reinvigorated democracy. He transformed the country.

And that is what we have to do today.

And, by the way, almost everything he proposed was called "socialist." Social Security, which transformed life for the elderly in this country was "socialist." The concept of the "minimum wage" was seen as a radical intrusion into the marketplace and was described as "socialist." Unemployment insurance, abolishing child labor, the 40-hour work week, collective bargaining, strong banking regulations, deposit insurance, and job programs that put millions of people to work were all described, in one way or another, as "socialist." Yet, these programs have become the fabric of our nation and the foundation of the middle class.

Thirty years later, in the 1960s, President Johnson passed Medicare and Medicaid to provide health care to millions of senior citizens and families with children, persons with disabilities and some of the most vulnerable people in this county. Once again these vitally important programs were derided by the right wing as socialist programs that were a threat to our American way of life.

That was then. Now is now.

Today, in 2015, despite the Wall Street crash of 2008, which drove this country into the worst economic downturn since the Depression, the American people are clearly better off economically than we were in 1937.

But, here is a very hard truth that we must acknowledge and address. Despite a huge increase in technology and productivity, despite major growth in the U.S. and global economy, tens of millions of American families continue to lack the basic necessities of life, while millions more struggle every day to provide a minimal standard of living for their families. The reality is that for the last 40 years the great middle class of this country has been in decline and faith in our political system is now extremely low.

The rich get much richer. Almost everyone else gets poorer. Super PACs funded by billionaires buy elections. Ordinary people don't vote. We have an economic and political crisis in this country and the same old, same old establishment politics and economics will not effectively address it.

If we are serious about transforming our country,

if we are serious about rebuilding the middle class, if we are serious about reinvigorating our democracy, we need to develop a political movement which, once again, is prepared to take on and defeat a ruling class whose greed is destroying our nation. The billionaire class cannot have it all. Our government belongs to all of us, and not just the one percent.

We need to create a culture which, as Pope Francis reminds us, cannot just be based on the worship of money. We must not accept a nation in which billionaires compete as to the size of their super-yachts, while children in America go hungry and veterans sleep out on the streets.

Today, in America, we are the wealthiest nation in the history of the world, but few Americans know that because so much of the new income and wealth goes to the people on top. In fact, over the last 30 years, there has been a massive transfer of wealth – trillions of wealth – going from the middle class to the top one-tenth of 1 percent – a handful of people who have seen a doubling of the percentage of the wealth they own over that period.

Unbelievably, and grotesquely, the top one-tenth of 1 percent owns nearly as much wealth as the bottom 90 percent.

Today, in America, millions of our people are

working two or three jobs just to survive. In fact, Americans work longer hours than do the people of any industrialized country. Despite the incredibly hard work and long hours of the American middle class, 58 percent of all new income generated today is going to the top one percent.

Today, in America, as the middle class continues to disappear, median family income, is $4,100 less than it was in 1999. The median male worker made over $700 less than he did 42 years ago, after adjusting for inflation. Last year, the median female worker earned more than $1,000 less than she did in 2007.

Today, in America, the wealthiest country in the history of the world, more than half of older workers have no retirement savings – zero – while millions of elderly and people with disabilities are trying to survive on $12,000 or $13,000 a year. From Vermont to California, older workers are scared to death. "How will I retire with dignity?," they ask?

Today, in America, nearly 47 million Americans are living in poverty and over 20 percent of our children, including 36 percent of African American children, are living in poverty — the highest rate of childhood poverty of nearly any major country on earth.

Today, in America, 29 million Americans have

no health insurance and even more are underinsured with outrageously high co-payments and deductibles. Further, with the United States paying the highest prices in the world for prescription drugs, 1 out of 5 patients cannot afford to fill the prescriptions their doctors write.

Today, in America, youth unemployment and underemployment is over 35 percent. Meanwhile, we have more people in jail than any other country and countless lives are being destroyed as we spend $80 billion a year locking up fellow Americans.

The bottom line is that today in America we not only have massive wealth and income inequality, but a power structure which protects that inequality. A handful of super-wealthy campaign contributors have enormous influence over the political process, while their lobbyists determine much of what goes on in Congress.

In 1944, in his State of the Union speech, President Roosevelt outlined what he called a second Bill of Rights. This is one of the most important speeches ever made by a president but, unfortunately, it has not gotten the attention that it deserves.

In that remarkable speech this is what Roosevelt stated, and I quote: "We have come to a clear realization of the fact that true individual freedom cannot exist without economic security and independence. Necessitous men are not free men." End of quote. In other words, real freedom must include economic security. That was Roosevelt's vision 70 years ago. It is my vision today. It is a vision that we have not yet achieved. It is time that we did.

In that speech, Roosevelt described the economic rights that he believed every American was entitled to: The right to a decent job at decent pay, the right to adequate food, clothing, and time off from work, the right for every business, large and small, to function in an atmosphere free from unfair competition and domination by monopolies. The right of all Americans to have a decent home and decent health care.

What Roosevelt was stating in 1944, what Martin Luther King, Jr. stated in similar terms 20 years later and what I believe today, is that true freedom does not occur without economic security.

People are not truly free when they are unable to feed their family. People are not truly free when they are unable to retire with dignity. People are not truly free when they are unemployed or underpaid or when they are exhausted by working long hours. People are not truly free when they have no health care.

So let me define for you, simply and straightforwardly, what democratic socialism means to me. It builds on what Franklin Delano Roosevelt said when he fought for guaranteed economic rights for all Americans. And it builds on what Martin Luther King, Jr. said in 1968 when he stated that; "This country has socialism for the rich, and rugged individualism for the poor." It builds on the success of many other countries around the world that have done a far better job than we have in protecting the needs of their working families, the elderly, the children, the sick and the poor.

Democratic socialism means that we must create an economy that works for all, not just the very wealthy.

Democratic socialism means that we must reform a political system in America today which is not only grossly unfair but, in many respects, corrupt.

It is a system, for example, which during the 1990s allowed Wall Street to spend $5 billion in lobbying and campaign contributions to get deregulated. Then, ten years later, after the greed, recklessness, and illegal behavior of Wall Street led to their collapse, it is a system which provided trillions in government aid to bail them out. Wall Street used their wealth and power to get Congress to do their bidding for deregulation and then, when their greed caused their collapse, they used their wealth and power to get Congress to bail them out. Quite a system!

And, then, to add insult to injury, we were told that not only were the banks too big to fail, the bankers were too big to jail. Kids who get caught possessing marijuana get police records. Wall Street CEOs who help destroy the economy get raises in their salaries. This is what Martin Luther King, Jr. meant by socialism for the rich and rugged individualism for everyone else.

In my view, it's time we had democratic socialism for working families, not just Wall Street, billionaires and large corporations. It means that we should not be providing welfare for corporations, huge tax breaks for the very rich, or trade policies which boost corporate profits as workers lose their jobs. It means that we create a government that works for works for all of us, not just powerful special interests. It means that economic rights must be an essential part of what America stands for.

It means that health care should be a right of all people, not a privilege. This is not a radical idea. It exists in every other major country on earth. Not just Denmark, Sweden or Finland. It exists in Canada, France, Germany and Taiwan. That is why I believe in a Medicare-for-all single payer health care system. Yes. The Affordable Care Act, which I helped write and voted for, is a step forward for this country. But we must build on it and go further.

Medicare for all would not only guarantee health care for all people, not only save middle class families and our entire nation significant sums of money, it would radically improve the lives of all Americans and bring about significant improvements in our economy.

People who get sick will not have to worry about paying a deductible or making a co-payment. They could go to the doctor when they should, and not end up in the emergency room. Business owners will not have to spend enormous amounts of time worrying about how they are going to provide health care for their employees. Workers will not have to be trapped in jobs they do not like simply because their employers are offering them decent health insurance plans. Instead, they will be able to pursue the jobs and work they love, which could be an enormous boon for the economy. And by the way, moving to a Medicare for all program will end the disgrace of Americans paying, by far, the highest prices in the world for prescription drugs.

Democratic socialism means that, in the year 2015, a college degree is equivalent to what a high school degree was 50 years ago – and that public education must allow every person in this country, who has the ability, the qualifications and the desire, the right to go to a public colleges or university tuition free. This is also not a radical idea. It exists today in many countries around the world. In fact, it used to exist in the United States.

Democratic socialism means that our government does everything it can to create a full employment economy. It makes far more sense to put millions of people back to work rebuilding our crumbling infrastructure, than to have a real unemployment rate of almost 10%. It is far smarter to invest in jobs and educational opportunities for unemployed young people, than to lock them up and spend $80 billion a year through mass incarceration.

Democratic socialism means that if someone works forty hours a week, that person should not be living in poverty: that we must raise the minimum wage to a living wage – $15 an hour over the next few years. It means that we join the rest of the world and pass the very strong Paid Family and Medical Leave legislation now in Congress. How can it possibly be that the United States, today, is virtually the only nation on earth, large or small, which does not guarantee that a working class woman can stay home for a reasonable period of time with her new-born baby? How absurd is that?

Democratic socialism means that we have government policy which does not allow the greed and profiteering of the fossil fuel industry to destroy our environment and our planet, and that we have a moral responsibility to combat climate change and leave this planet healthy and habitable for our kids and grandchildren.

Democratic socialism means, that in a democratic, civilized society the wealthiest people and the largest corporations must pay their fair share of taxes. Yes. Innovation, entrepreneurship and business success should be rewarded. But greed for the sake of greed is not something that public policy should support. It is not acceptable that in a rigged economy in the last two years the wealthiest 15 Americans saw their wealth increase by $170 billion, more wealth than is owned by the bottom 130 million Americans. Let us not forget what Pope Francis has so elegantly stated; "We have created new idols. The worship of the golden calf of old has found a new and heartless image in the cult of money and the dictatorship of an economy which is faceless and lacking any truly humane goal."

It is not acceptable that major corporations stash their profits in the Cayman Islands and other offshore tax havens to avoid paying $100 billion in taxes each and every year. It is not acceptable that hedge fund managers pay a lower effective tax rate than nurses or truck drivers. It is not acceptable that billionaire families are able to leave virtually all of their wealth to their families without paying a reasonable estate tax. It is not acceptable that Wall Street speculators are able to gamble trillions of dollars in the derivatives market without paying a nickel in taxes on those transactions.

Democratic socialism, to me, does not just mean that we must create a nation of economic and social justice. It also means that we must create a vibrant democracy based on the principle of one person one vote. It is extremely sad that the United States, one of the oldest democracies on earth, has one of the lowest voter turnouts of any major country, and that millions of young and working class people have given up on our political system entirely. Every American should be embarrassed that in our last national election 63% of the American people, and 80% of young people, did not vote. Clearly, despite the efforts of many Republican governors to suppress the vote, we must make it easier for people to participate in the political process, not harder. It is not too much to demand that everyone 18 years of age is registered to vote – end of discussion.

Further, it is unacceptable that we have a corrupt campaign finance system which allows millionaires, billionaires and large corporations to contribute as much as they want to Super Pacs to elect candidates who will represent their special interests. We must overturn Citizens United and move to public funding of elections.

So the next time you hear me attacked as a socialist, remember this:

I don't believe government should own the means of production, but I do believe that the middle class and the working families who produce the wealth of America deserve a fair deal.

I believe in private companies that thrive and invest and grow in America instead of shipping jobs and profits overseas.

I believe that most Americans can pay lower taxes – if hedge fund managers who make billions manipulating the marketplace finally pay the taxes they should.

I don't believe in special treatment for the top 1%, but I do believe in equal treatment for African-Americans who are right to proclaim the moral principle that Black Lives Matter.

I despise appeals to nativism and prejudice, and I do believe in immigration reform that gives Hispanics and others a pathway to citizenship and a better life.

I don't believe in some foreign "ism", but I believe deeply in American idealism.

I'm not running for president because it's my turn, but because it's the turn of all of us to live in a nation of hope and opportunity not for some, not for the few, but for all.

No one understood better than FDR the connection between American strength at home and our ability to defend America at home and across the world. That is why he proposed a second Bill of Rights in 1944, and said in that State of the Union:

"America's own rightful place in the world depends in large part upon how fully these and similar rights have been carried into practice for all our citizens. For unless there is security here at home there cannot be lasting peace in the world."

I'm not running to pursue reckless adventures abroad, but to rebuild America's strength at home. I will never hesitate to defend this nation, but I will never send our sons and daughters to war under false pretense or pretenses or into dubious battles with no end in sight.

And when we discuss foreign policy, let me join the people of Paris in mourning their loss, and pray that those who have been wounded will enjoy a full recovery. Our hearts also go out to the families of the hundreds of Russians apparently killed by an ISIS bomb on their flight, and those who lost their lives to terrorist attacks in Lebanon and elsewhere.

To my mind, it is clear that the United States must pursue policies to destroy the brutal and barbaric ISIS regime, and to create conditions that prevent fanatical extremist ideologies from flourishing. But we cannot – and should not – do it alone.

Our response must begin with an understanding of past mistakes and missteps in our previous approaches to foreign policy. It begins with the acknowledgment that unilateral military action should be a last resort, not a first resort, and that ill-conceived military decisions, such as the invasion of Iraq, can wreak far-reaching devastation and destabilize entire regions for decades. It begins with the reflection that the failed policy decisions of the past – rushing to war, regime change in Iraq, or toppling Mossadegh in Iran in 1953, or Guatemalan President Árbenz in 1954, Brazilian President Goulart in 1964, Chilean President Allende in 1973. These are the sorts of policies do not work, do not make us safer, and must not be repeated.

After World War II, in response to the fear of Soviet aggression, European nations and the United States established the North Atlantic Treaty Organization – an organization based on shared interests and goals and the notion of a collective defense against a common enemy. It is my belief that we must expand on these ideals and solidify our commitments to work together to combat the global threat of terror.

We must create an organization like NATO to confront the security threats of the 21st century – an organization that emphasizes cooperation and collaboration to defeat the rise of violent extremism and importantly to address the root causes underlying these brutal acts. We must work with our NATO partners, and expand our coalition to include Russia and members of the Arab League.

But let's be very clear. While the U.S. and other western nations have the strength of our militaries and political systems, the fight against ISIS is a struggle for the soul of Islam, and countering violent extremism and destroying ISIS must be done primarily by Muslim nations – with the strong support of their global partners.

These same sentiments have been echoed by those in the region. Jordan's King Abdallah II said in a speech on Sunday that terrorism is the "greatest threat to our region" and that Muslims must lead the fight against it. He noted that confronting extremism is both a regional and international responsibility, and that it is incumbent on Muslim nations and communities to confront those who seek to hijack their societies and generations with intolerance and violent ideology.

And let me congratulate King Abdallah not only for his wise remarks, but also for the role that his small country is playing in attempting to address the horrific refugee crisis in the region.

A new and strong coalition of Western powers, Muslim nations, and countries like Russia must come together in a strongly coordinated way to combat ISIS, to seal the borders that fighters are currently flowing across, to share counter-terrorism intelligence, to turn off the spigot of terrorist financing, and to end support for exporting radical ideologies.

What does all of this mean? Well, it means that, in many cases, we must ask more from those in the region. While Jordan, Turkey, Egypt, and Lebanon have accepted their responsibilities for taking in Syrian refugees, other countries in the region have done nothing or very little.

Equally important, and this is a point that must be made – countries in the region like Saudi Arabia, Kuwait, Qatar, UAE – countries of enormous wealth and resources – have contributed far too little in the fight against ISIS. That must change. King Abdallah is absolutely right when he says that that the Muslim nations must lead the fight against ISIS, and that includes some of the most wealthy and powerful nations in the region, who, up to this point have done far too little.

Saudi Arabia has the 3rd largest defense budget in the world, yet instead of fighting ISIS they have focused more on a campaign to oust Iran-backed Houthi rebels in Yemen. Kuwait, a country whose ruling family was restored to power by U.S. troops after the first Gulf War, has been a well-known source of financing for ISIS and other violent extremists. It has been reported that Qatar will spend $200 billion on the 2022 World Cup, including the construction of an enormous number of facilities to host that event – $200 billion on hosting a soccer event, yet very little to fight against ISIS. Worse still, it has been widely reported that the government has not been vigilant in stemming the flow of terrorist financing, and that Qatari individuals and organizations funnel money to some of the most extreme terrorist groups, including al Nusra and ISIS.

All of this has got to change. Wealthy and powerful Muslim nations in the region can no longer sit on the sidelines and expect the United States to do their work for them. As we develop a strongly coordinated effort, we need a commitment from these countries that the fight against ISIS takes precedence over the religious and ideological differences that hamper the kind of cooperation that we desperately need.

Further, we all understand that Bashar al-Assad is a brutal dictator who has slaughtered many of his own people. I am pleased that we saw last weekend diplomats from all over world, known as the International Syria Support Group, set a timetable for a Syrian-led political transition with open and fair elections. These are the promising beginnings of a collective effort to end the bloodshed and to move to political transition.

The diplomatic plan for Assad's transition from power is a good step in a united front. But our priority must be to defeat ISIS. Nations all over the world, who share a common interest in protecting themselves against international terrorist, must make the destruction of ISIS the highest priority. Nations in the region must commit – that instead of turning a blind eye — they will commit their resources to preventing the free flow of terrorist finances and fighters to Syria and Iraq. We need a commitment that they will counter the violent rhetoric that fuels terrorism – rhetoric that often occurs within their very borders.

This is the model in which we must pursue solutions to the sorts of global threats we face.

While individual nations indeed have historic disputes – the U.S. and Russia, Iran and Saudi Arabia – the time is now to put aside those differences to work towards a common purpose of destroying ISIS. Sadly, as we have seen recently, no country is immune from attacks by the violent organization or those whom they have radicalized.

Thus, we must work with our partners in Europe, the Gulf states, Africa, and Southeast Asia – all along the way asking the hard questions whether their actions are serving our unified purpose.

The bottom line is that ISIS must be destroyed, but it cannot be defeated by the United States alone. A new and effective coalition must be formed with the Muslim nations leading the effort on the ground, while the United States and other major forces provide the support they need.

CHAPTER 7
S.C.L. Conference
July 25, 2015

Thank you for inviting me to be with you tonight. Thank you for the work you continue to do as leaders in civil rights. You have always been a voice for the voiceless and champions for social justice.

Your courageous history dates back to the Montgomery Bus Boycott when one person, Rosa Parks, by the simple act of sitting down at the front of the bus, inspired a whole community to stand up and bring the transportation system in Montgomery to its knees, to capture the imagination of the nation and to cause what my friend John Lewis calls "a nonviolent revolution."

You knew then, what the American people are beginning to remember now – that real change takes place when millions of people stand up and say "enough is enough," and when we create a political revolution from the ground up. That is what the Southern Christian Leadership Conference has always been about. That is what is beginning to happen today. The American people are sick and tired with establishment politics, with establishment economics and with establishment media. They're sick of being told that they don't matter. They fully understand that corporate greed is destroying our economy, that

American politics is now dominated by a handful of billionaires and that much of the corporate media is prepared to discuss everything except the most important issues facing our country.

I realize that many of you don't know me very well. So let me take a moment to let you know a little bit about my background. I was mayor of Burlington, Vermont, from 1981-1989, Vermont's lone congressman from 1990-2006 and a U.S. senator from Vermont from 2007 until today.

I was born in Brooklyn, New York. My father came to this country from Poland at the age of 17 without a penny in his pocket and without much of an education. My mother graduated from high school in New York City. My father worked for almost his entire life as a paint salesman and we lived with my brother in a small rent-controlled apartment. My mother's dream was to move out of that three-room apartment into a home of our own. She died young and her dream was never fulfilled. As a kid I learned what lack of money means to a family, a lesson I have never forgotten.

When I was a young college student, I came to Washington, D.C., to participate in the March on Washington for Jobs and Freedom. I heard this organization's first president, the Rev. Martin Luther King Jr., deliver his famous speech, and he inspired me, just as he inspired a whole generation – black and white – to get involved in the civil rights movement. In Chicago, I worked for housing desegregation and was arrested protesting public school segregation. During that time I was active in what was a sister-organization to the SCLC, the Congress of Racial Equality of CORE, which was headed up by the late James Farmer.

Since I have been an elected official, I have used my influence to stand with those who have no power, and to take on virtually every element of our current ruling class – from Wall Street, to the insurance companies, to the drug companies to Big Energy, to the Koch Brothers to the Military Industrial Complex. That's what I do.

The decision to run for president was a very difficult one for me and my family. I love my job as Vermont's senator and love spending time in Vermont with my four kids and seven beautiful grandchildren – something, needless to say, that I am less able to do today.

My family and I decided that I should run for president because the reality is that this country today faces more serious problems than at any time since the Great Depression and, if you include the planetary crisis of climate change, it may well be that the challenges we face now are more dire than any time in our modern history. And to address these crises we need leadership that is prepared to rally the American people, to create the political revolution that this country desperately needs, to take on the wealthy special interests that wield so much power.

Let me take this opportunity to quote from an excellent article by the columnist Eugene Robinson which appeared in the Washington Post. Here are some excerpts from that article:

As we celebrate King's great achievement and sacrifice, it is wrong to round off the sharp edges of his legacy. He saw inequality as a fundamental and tragic flaw in this society, and he made clear in the weeks leading up to his assassination that economic issues were becoming the central focus of his advocacy.

Nearly five decades later, King's words on the subject still ring true. On March 10, 1968, just weeks before his death, he spoke to a union group in New York about what he called "the other America." He was preparing to launch a Poor People's Campaign whose premise was that issues of jobs and issues of justice were inextricably intertwined.

"One America is flowing with the milk of prosperity and the honey of equality," King said. "That America is the habitat of millions of people who have food and material necessities for their bodies, culture and education for their minds, freedom and human dignity for their spirits. . . . But as we assemble here tonight, I'm sure that each of us is painfully aware of the fact that there is another America, and that other America has a daily ugliness about it that transforms the buoyancy of hope into the fatigue of despair."

Those who lived in the other America, King said, were plagued by "inadequate, substandard and often dilapidated housing conditions," by "substandard, inferior, quality-less schools," by having to choose between unemployment and low-wage jobs that didn't even pay enough to put food on the table.

The problem was structural, King said: "This country has socialism for the rich, rugged individualism for the poor."

Eight days later, speaking in Memphis, King continued the theme. "Do you know that most of the poor people in our country are working every day?" he asked striking sanitation workers. "And they are making wages so low that they cannot begin to function in the mainstream of the economic life of our nation. These are facts which must be seen, and it is criminal to have people working on a full-time basis and a full-time job getting part-time income."

King explained the shift in his focus: "Now our

struggle is for genuine equality, which means economic equality. For we know that it isn't enough to integrate lunch counters. What does it profit a man to be able to eat at an integrated lunch counter if he doesn't earn enough money to buy a hamburger and a cup of coffee?"

But what King saw in 1968 — and what we all should recognize today — is that it is useless to try to address race without also taking on the larger issue of inequality. He was planning a poor people's march on Washington that would include not only African-Americans but also Latinos, Native Americans and poor Appalachian whites. He envisioned a rainbow of the dispossessed, assembled to demand not just an end to discrimination but a change in the way the economy doles out its spoils."

And that is the theme that I wish to pursue this evening. The need to simultaneously address the structural and institutional racism which exists in this country, while at the same time we vigorously attack the grotesque level of income and wealth inequality which is making the very rich much richer while everyone else – especially the African-American community and working-class whites – are becoming poorer.

Let's go to an issue that is rightly on everyone's mind, the continuing struggle for racial justice in

America and the need to combat structural racism. Let's start with the facts. The horrible facts.

If current trends continue, one in four black males born today can expect to spend time in prison during their lifetime. This is an unspeakable tragedy.

Blacks are imprisoned at six times the rate of whites.

People of color are incarcerated, policed and sentenced to death at significantly higher rates than their white counterparts.

One in every 15 African-American men is incarcerated, compared to one in every 106 white men.

A report by the Department of Justice found that blacks were three times more likely to be searched during a traffic stop, compared to white motorists.

African-Americans are twice as likely to be arrested and almost four times as likely to experience the use of force during encounters with the police.

African-Americans make up two-fifths of confined youth today.

African-American women are three times more likely than white women to be incarcerated.

Once convicted, black offenders receive longer sentences (10 percent longer) than white offenders for the same crimes.

Thirteen percent of African-American men have lost the right to vote due to felony convictions.

But as bad as those statistics are, and they are indeed a tragedy, the situation for many people of color is worse yet.

Too many African-Americans today are simultaneously having to deal the crisis of racial justice while coping with the effects of poverty and economic deprivation, such as drugs, crime, and despair.

Of course the majority of people of color are trying to work hard, play by the rules and raise their children. But there are neighborhoods where mothers are afraid to let their children outside for fear of gang violence and drugs. And they are also afraid of their children being targeted by the police because of the color of their skin. No person should have to worry that a routine interaction with law enforcement will end in violence or death.

As Martin Luther King, Jr., said; Law and order exist for the purpose of establishing justice and when they fail in this purpose they become the dangerously structured dams that block the flow of social progress.

Across the nation, too many African-Americans and other minorities find themselves subjected to a system that treats citizens who have not committed crimes like criminals. A growing number of communities do not trust the police and police have become disconnected from the communities they are sworn to protect.

Sandra Bland, Michael Brown, Rekia Boyd, Eric Garner, Walter Scott, Freddie Gray, Tamir Rice. We know their names. Each of them died unarmed at the hands of police officers or in police custody. The chants are growing louder. People are angry. I am angry. And people have a right to be angry. Violence and brutality of any kind, particularly at the hands of law enforcement sworn to protect and serve our communities, is unacceptable and must not be tolerated.

We must reform our criminal justice system. Black lives do matter. And we must value black lives.

We must move away from the militarization of police forces. We must invest in community policing. Only when we get officers into the communities, working within the neighborhoods before trouble arises, do we really develop the relationships necessary to make our communities safer.

We need a federal initiative to completely redo how we train police officers in this country and give them body cameras. States and localities that make progress in this area should get more federal justice grant money. Those that do not should get their funding slashed. The measure of success for law enforcement should not be how many people get locked up.

For people who have committed crimes that have landed them in jail, there needs to be a path back from prison. The federal system of parole needs to be reinstated. We need real education and real skills training for the incarcerated.

We must end the over incarceration of non-violent young Americans who do not pose a serious threat to our society. It is an international embarrassment that we have more people locked up in jail than any other country on earth – more than even the Communist totalitarian state of China. That has got to end.

The war on drugs has been a failure and has ruined the lives of too many people. African-Americans comprise 14 percent of regular drug users but are 37 percent of those arrested for drug offenses. From 1980 to 2007, about one in three adults arrested for drugs was African-American.

It is an obscenity that we stigmatize so many

young Americans with a criminal record for smoking marijuana, but not one major Wall Street executive has been prosecuted for causing the near collapse of our entire economy. This must change.

We need to end prisons for profit, which result in an over-incentive to arrest, jail and detain, in order to keep prison beds full. We need to invest in drug courts and medical and mental health interventions for people with substance abuse problems, so that they do not end up in prison, they end up in treatment.

But we have to go beyond just violence perpetuated by the state. As we saw so horribly in South Carolina, there are still those who seek to terrorize the African American community with violence and intimidation. We need to make sure the federal resources are there to crack down on the illegal activities of hate groups. We need a new social movement to let all the racist haters out there know that they will no longer be accepted in a civilized society.

In addition to the physical violence faced by too many in our country we need look at the lives of black children and address a few other difficult facts. Black children, who make up just 18 percent of preschoolers, account for 48 percent of all out-of-school suspensions before kindergarten. We are failing our black children before kindergarten! Black students were expelled at three times the rate of white students. Black girls were suspended at higher rates than all other girls and most boys. According to the Department of Education, African American students are more likely to suffer harsh punishments – suspensions and arrests – at school.

We need to take a hard look at education system. Black students attended schools with higher concentrations of first-year teachers, compared with white students. Black students were more than three times as likely to attend schools where fewer than 60 percent of teachers meet all state certification and licensure requirements.

We must get into our schools and keep kids in school. We must ensure that children graduate from high school and don't drop out. This is a complicated problem and I'm not going to stand here and say I have all the answers.

But one thing that will help kids stay in school is if they have a belief that they will be able to get a college education. For too many families college seems like an impossibility. We have got to change that. We need to give our children, regardless of their race or their income, a fair shot at attending college. That's why I support making all public universities tuition free.

Communities of color also face the violence of economic deprivation. Let's be frank: neighborhoods like those in west Baltimore, where Freddie Gray resided, suffer the most. However, the problem of economic immobility isn't just a problem for young men like Freddie Gray. It has become a problem for millions of Americans who, despite hard-work and the will to get ahead, can spend their entire lives struggling to survive on the economic treadmill.

We live at a time when most Americans don't have $10,000 in savings, and millions of working adults have no idea how they will ever retire in dignity. God forbid, they are confronted with an unforeseen car accident, a medical emergency, or the loss of a job. It would literally send their lives into an economic tailspin. And the problems are even more serious when we consider race.

Most black and Latino households have less than $350 in savings. The black unemployment rate has remained roughly twice as high as the white rate over the last 40 years, regardless of education. This is unacceptable. The American people in general, want change – they want a better deal. A fairer deal. A new deal. They want an America with laws and policies that truly reward hard work with economic mobility. They want an America that affords all of its citizens with the economic security to take risks and the opportunity to realize their full potential.

Today, we live in the wealthiest nation in the history of the world, but that reality means little because almost all of that wealth is controlled by a tiny handful of individuals.

There is something profoundly wrong when the top one-tenth of 1 percent owns almost as much wealth as the bottom 90 percent, and when 99 percent of all new income goes to the top 1 percent. There is something profoundly wrong when we have a proliferation of millionaires and billionaires at the same time as millions of Americans work longer hours for lower wages and we have the highest rate of childhood poverty of any major country on earth. There is something profoundly wrong when one family owns more wealth than the bottom 130 million Americans. This grotesque level of inequality is immoral. It is bad economics. It is unsustainable. That is why we need a tax system that is fair and progressive, which makes wealthy individuals and profitable corporations begin to pay their fair share of taxes. This type of rigged economy is not what America is supposed to be about. This has got to change and, together we will change it.

We need to send a message to the billionaire class: "You can't have it all. You can't get huge tax breaks while children in this country go hungry. You can't continue sending our jobs to China while millions are looking for work. You can't hide your profits in the Cayman Islands and other tax havens, while there are massive unmet needs on every corner of this nation. Your greed has got to end. You cannot take advantage of all the benefits of America, if you refuse to accept your responsibilities as Americans."

But it is not just income and wealth inequality. It is the tragic reality that for the last 40 years the great middle class of our country – once the envy of the world – has been disappearing. Despite exploding technology and increased worker productivity, median family income is almost $5,000 less than it was in 1999. Throughout this country it is not uncommon for people to be working two or three jobs just to cobble together enough income and some health care benefits to survive.

The truth is that real unemployment is not the 5.5 percent you read in newspapers. It is close to 11 percent if you include those workers who have given up looking for jobs or who are working part-time when they want to work full-time. And here is something we don't hear much about. According to a recent analysis of Census Bureau data by the Economic Policy Institute, real youth unemployment in this country has reached crisis proportions. If you include those who are not working, who have given up looking for work or who are working part-time, white high school graduates aged 17-20 have an unemployment rate of 33 percent, Hispanics in the same age group have an unemployment rate of 36 percent while black youth have an unemployment rate of 51 percent. Today, shamefully, we have 45 million people living in poverty, many of whom are working at low-wage jobs.

Let us be honest and acknowledge that millions of Americans are now working for totally inadequate wages. The current federal minimum wage of $7.25 an hour is a starvation wage and must be raised. The minimum wage must become a living wage – which means raising it to $15 an hour over the next few years. The benchmark of full time work in America should be simple and concrete – that no full-time worker should live in poverty.

And a living wage should not only be fair, it should be equitable. That is why we must establish pay equity for women workers by law. It's unconscionable that women earn 78 cents on the dollar compared to men who perform the same work. We must also end the scandal in which millions of American employees, often earning less than $30,000 a year, work 50 or 60 hours a week – and earn no overtime.

Further, the United States must end the international embarrassment of being the only major country on earth, the only one, which does not guarantee workers paid medical and family leave, paid sick time and paid vacation time. Last place is no place for America. That is why I will fight for 12 weeks of paid family leave, at least 10 days of paid vacation time and seven days of paid sick time. My Republican colleagues talk a lot about "family values." Well, let me be very clear. It is not a family value to force the mother of a new born baby to go back to work a few days after she gives birth, because she doesn't have the money to stay home and bond with her baby. That is not a family value. That is an insult to everything that I know about what family is about.

Today, as a result of the collapse of our middle class and declining wages, the American people are working longer hours than the people of any other country – 137 hours a year more than the Japanese, 260 more hours per year than the British and 499 hours a year more than the French. Well, 100 years later we still have not achieved that. Incredibly, today, 85 percent of working men and 66 percent of working women work more than 40 hours a week. And do you know what? Many workers in this country get no or very little paid vacation time. That has got to end.

At a time when millions of Americans are struggling to keep their heads above water economically, at a time when senior poverty is increasing, at a time when millions of kids are living in dire poverty my Republican colleagues are trying to make a terrible situation even worse. If you can believe it, the Republican budget throws 27 million Americans off health insurance, makes drastic cuts in Medicare, throws millions of low income Americans, including pregnant women off nutrition programs, and makes it harder for working-class families to afford college or put their kids into Head Start. And then, to add insult to injury, they provide huge tax breaks for the very, very wealthiest families in this country while they raise taxes on working families.

Well, let me tell my Republican colleagues that I respectfully disagree with their approach. Instead of cutting Social Security, we need to expand Social Security benefits. Instead of cutting Head Start and childcare, we need to move to a universal pre-k system for all the children of this country. As Franklin Delano Roosevelt reminded us: "The test of our progress is not whether we add more to the abundance of those who have much, it is whether we provide enough for those who have little." And that is a test that we as a nation must once again meet and master.

We need to make health care a basic right in our society.

We need to make sure every parent has quality affordable child care and where all of our qualified young people, regardless of income, can go to college, by making a 4-year education at every public college and university in this country free. If Germany, Sweden and Denmark can afford to do this, then so can we.

We need to invest in jobs and job training, rather than to be building more and more jails and to be locking up more and more people. That is why I have submitted legislation to spend $5.5 billion dollars to fund job-training programs for inner city youth. Instead of building more and more prisons, we need to be building more and more meaningful lives where young people can have a future, not be stuck in a dead end with no hope or opportunity.

If we are serious about reversing the decline of the middle class we need a major federal jobs program that puts millions of Americans back to work at decent paying jobs. At a time when our roads, bridges, water systems, rail and airports are decaying, the most effective way to rapidly create meaningful jobs is to rebuild our crumbling infrastructure. That's why I've introduced legislation that would invest $1 trillion over 5 years to modernize our country's physical infrastructure. This legislation would create and maintain at least 13 million good-paying jobs, while making our country more productive, efficient and safe. And I commit to you that as president, I will lead that legislation into law.

This is an ambitious program that would lift millions of families out of poverty and provide a pathway to greater economic security for all Americans. The right to a college education, the right to health care, and a guaranteed right to employment. It will not heal all wounds or relieve all tensions, but it would go beyond anything we have tried before, and it would send a clear signal that black lives matter.

I want to talk about our democracy. The billionaire class is controlling our political and economic lives because of the disastrous Citizens United case. The Supreme Court unconscionably gutted the Voting Rights Act. Make no mistake, we watching the erosion of our democracy and the gains that we have fought so hard to achieve.

Some of you may not see the connection between an out-of-control campaign financing system and the gutting of our voting rights, but you should not be fooled – they are two sides of the same coin. Our access to our democracy is being ripped away. The billionaires do not want people to vote.

My friends – let me be as blunt as I can while telling you what you already know. As a result of the disastrous Supreme Court decision in the Citizens United case, the American political system has been totally corrupted, and the foundations of American democracy are being undermined. What the Supreme

Court essentially said was that it was not good enough for the billionaire class to own much of our economy. They could now own the U.S. government as well. And that is precisely what they are trying to do.

If we are serious about creating jobs, about climate change and the needs of our children, our veterans and the elderly, about reforming our criminal justice system, we must be deadly serious about campaign finance reform. That is why in my campaign for president, I have said that I will not nominate any justice to the Supreme Court who has not made it clear that he or she will move to overturn that disastrous decision which is undermining our democracy. Long term, we need to go further and establish public funding of elections, so that the dark money of American politics is stopped before democracy is bought and paid for by a handful of billionaires and corporations.

American democracy is not about corporations and billionaires being able to buy candidates and elections. It is not about Wall Street and big oil or the Koch brothers and Sheldon Adelson spending billions of dollars to elect candidates who will make the rich richer and everyone else poorer. According to media reports the Koch brothers alone, one family, will spend more money in this election cycle than either the Democratic or Republican parties. This is not democracy. This is oligarchy. The defining principle of American democracy is one person, one vote – with every citizen having an equal say – and no voter suppression. And that's the kind of American political system we have to fight for.

Not only are big moneyed interests trying to buy the American electorate, Republican-controlled legislatures have done everything in their power to make it more difficult to vote.

Voting is becoming more difficult, not less. The Voting Rights Act has been gutted by the Supreme Court, and efforts to repair it in Congress have been sidelined. Voter suppression today is alive and well in the form of unnecessary voter ID laws, restrictions on registering to vote, improper purging of voter rolls, felon disenfranchisement, and a staggering array of deceptive practices that are preventing eligible voters from participating in the political process. It is embarrassing that the United States' voting system is so dysfunctional.

We need to remember the price that was paid for the right to vote. We must restore our democracy's promise of one man, one vote. We must repeal Citizens United and take the political process back from the billionaire class. We need to extend early voting, extend voting hours, make Election Day a holiday or move it to a weekend.

One area that I have been interested in is voter

registration. Unsurprisingly, most other advanced democracies make voter registration much easier than we do here in the United States. Some countries, such as Argentina, Belgium, and Germany, maintain a national or municipal population database and local election officials add eligible voters to the rolls based on those lists. Some countries hire workers to go door-to-door and register all eligible voters, including Great Britain and Indonesia. Mexico deploys such workers to rural areas.

France automatically registers 18-year-olds to vote when they register with the Selective Service. Canada uses info collected from other government agencies to add eligible citizens to the rolls—British Columbia uses DMV records; Quebec uses health insurance records. If more info is needed, the government reaches out by mail and sends the potential voter a registration form, with a postage-paid return envelope.

The U.S. is one of the few countries which puts the onus of registration on the voter, not the state. This is ridiculous.

In 2009, the Brennan Center released a study of worldwide voter registration rates, based on citizen voting-age population. Here are a few countries:

Argentina (2007): 100%
Great Britain (2008): 97%
Belgium (2007): 94%
Canada (2008): 93%
Germany (2005): 93%
Australia (2008): 92%
France (2007): 91%
United States (2006): 68%

The Census Bureau Population Survey says in 2012, 71.2 percent of Americans were registered to vote. The number varies by age—only 58 percent of 18-29-year-olds were registered to vote, but 79 percent of those older than 70 were registered.

We should be making voting easier, not harder.

Let us also be very clear that the stakes are very high. The right to vote is preservative of all other rights. And when in this last election in November 63 percent of the American people chose not to vote; 80 percent of young people chose not to vote; and almost 75 percent of low-income workers chose not to vote, it should not come as a surprise that the stranglehold that the billionaire class has on the economy is tightening around the middle class.

And when we talk about voting rights, we have to address the reality of over 2 million African-Americans who have been disenfranchised due to criminal convictions. This is not the way to help bring people returning from prison back into their communities. If you can believe it, in some states over 20 percent of the African-American population is disenfranchised. Florida – 23 percent. Virginia – 20 percent. Kentucky – 22 percent. But the percentages don't necessarily give the entire picture because in many, many states with large African American populations, the percentage may be lower but the number of individuals who can't cast a ballot is high. Georgia – almost 160,000 people; Texas – over 150,000 people; Alabama – over 135,000 people; Mississippi – over 107,000 people. That is why I am a sponsor of legislation introduced on the House side by Rep. John Conyers called the Democracy Restoration Act which would restore federal voting rights.

We must remember that the struggle for our rights is not a struggle for one day, or one year, or one generation – it is the struggle of a lifetime, and one that must be fought by every generation.

All of you in this room know it, but it bears saying out loud: civil rights are not just about for voting rights, but economic and social equality – and most importantly, jobs. 50 years later, it remains the great unfinished business of the civil rights movement.

In conclusion, I've been traveling this country for over a year now. People are ready for a new movement – a political revolution – to transform our country economically, politically, socially and environmentally. In other words, we are building a movement of millions of Americans who are prepared to stand up and fight back.

I believe the time has come to say loudly and clearly: enough is enough. This great nation and its government belong to all of the people, and not to a handful of billionaires, their Super-PACs and their lobbyists.

Now is not the time for thinking small. Now is not the time for the same-old, same-old establishment politics and stale inside-the-beltway ideas.

Now is the time for millions of working families – black and white, Latino and Native American, gay and straight – to come together, to revitalize American democracy, to end the collapse of the American middle class and to make certain that our children and grandchildren are able to enjoy a quality of life that brings them health, prosperity, security and joy – and that once again makes the United States the leader in the world in the fight for economic and social justice, for environmental sanity and for a world of peace.

CHAPTER 8
National Council of La Raza

August 12, 2015

These are tough times for our country and it is absolutely essential that we involve more people in the political process and that we provide a voice for those people who have no voice, for those people who are in the shadows, and that we engage in serious debate on serious issues and that is exactly what La Raza has been doing and will do and I thank you very much for that.

This morning in the brief time that I have I want to focus on three issues: I want to talk about the stain of racism in this country, I want to talk about the need for real immigration reform and I want to talk about economic policies that address the grotesque level of income and wealth inequality in America and the need to create an economy that works for all of us and not just a handful of billionaires.

Brothers and sisters, throughout history, for whatever reason (and I'm not a psychiatrist) racism has been a stain on human existence. As Janet mentioned, I lost many members of my family in Europe to Hitler and we know that all over this world including the United States, including North America, racism has existed and has done terrible, terrible things. And this issue was raised, interestingly enough, just a few days ago when Pope Francis, one of the very great leaders in this world today, stated and I quote "I humbly ask forgiveness, not only for the offense of the church herself, but also for crimes committed against the native peoples during the so-called conquest of America."

Racism has plagued the United States since its inception. The atrocities committed against the native people are unspeakable as is the abomination of slavery perpetrated against people of African descent. Millions of people died as a result of that racism and that exploitation of one group of people thinking they are superior to another group of people because of differences of color or of language or of customs. But racism in our country has not only impacted Native Americans and African Americans as you all know, it has impacted people who've come to this country from Asia, from Ireland, from Italy, from countries from all over the world. Racism has plagued this country for centuries. We should be proud however, that in recent decades we have made significant progress, real progress in overcoming racism and in defeating it, in creating a country where we judge people, as Martin Luther King, Jr. reminded us, not on the color of their skin, not on the language they speak, not on the country where they came from, but on their character and qualities as human beings. We are making progress in this country and there will be no turning back and let me be very clear in stating that no one, not Donald Trump, not anyone else will be successful in dividing us based on race or our country of origin.

American becomes a greater nation, a stronger nation when we stand together as one people and in a very loud and clear voice we say no to all forms of racism and bigotry. As Janet mentioned, I know something about immigration because my Dad came to this country from Poland at the age of 17 without a nickel in his pocket, without much of an education and without knowing the English language. Like immigrants before and since, he worked hard to give his family a better life here in the United States. He never made much money. We lived in a three and a half room rent-controlled apartment in Brooklyn, New York but he worked hard, my mom worked hard and they were able to create a situation where their two kids went to college. Their story. my story, your story, our story is the story of America, hardworking families coming to the United States to create a brighter future for their kids. It is a story rooted in family and fueled by hope. It is a story that continues to this day in families all across the United States. My remarks this morning will focus on issues of specific relevance for the Latino community but also issues important to all Americans. But when we talk about the Latino community, and in fact when we talk about America, one critical piece that must be talked about is the need to enact comprehensive immigration reform.

Today we have 11 million people in this country who are undocumented, 99% of whom came to this country to improve their lives, to escape oppression, to flee desperate poverty and violence. Let us be frank, today's undocumented workers play an extraordinarily important role in our economy. Without these folks it is likely that our agricultural system would collapse. Undocumented workers are doing the extremely difficult work of harvesting our crops, building our homes, cooking our meals and caring for our children. They are part of the fabric of America.

Let me very briefly tell you my experience, one of my experiences with undocumented workers. In 2007 I heard about horrendous exploitation in Immokalee, Florida where undocumented workers grow tomatoes and on the day that I arrived in Immokalee, Florida, amazingly enough, the U.S. Attorney there was indicting some people on slavery, people being held in slavery, forced to work against their will. I saw the conditions of workers working horrendously long hours at very low wages, very bad working conditions, awful housing and I'm happy to say that with people working together we made some progress. Today workers there get better wages, get better working conditions and better housing.

Eleven million people came to this country, who are today undocumented so that they could feed their families, escape gang violence and desperate economic circumstances. Let me also be very clear, that people came to this country because they knew that there were jobs here and if anyone thinks that employers throughout this country did not know that the workers that they were hiring were undocumented, they know nothing about what has gone on in this country for 50 years.

So where do we go from here? Well, I supported the 2013 Comprehensive Immigration Reform Legislation in the U.S. Senate. While a complicated piece of comprehensive legislation like this can always be improved and should be improved, I believe there should be a responsible path to citizenship so individuals can come out of the shadows, people can walk the streets with safety, people can hold their heads high, so that people can have the protection of the law and participate fully and openly in American society. The Senate bill attempted to accomplish this important goal and the time is long overdue for the U.S. House of Representatives to take up immigration reform. The Senate bill contained the provisions of The DREAM Act which I strongly support and which would offer the opportunity of permanent residency and eventual citizenship to young people who are brought to the United States as children. It is my belief that we should recognize the young men and women who comprise the DREAMers for what they are, American kids who deserve the right to be in the country they know as home.

This is not to say that I do not have significant criticisms of this long and complicated bill. I believe the pathway to citizenship was unnecessarily linked to border security triggers, measures that many believe were put in place so that the path to citizenship would be delayed or even denied for the millions of undocumented individuals here and I want to change those provisions. I also believe that the penalties and fines in the bill would be a bar for the poor, essentially preventing them from accessing the path to legal residency and eventual citizenship. To be meaningful, a pathway to citizenship needs to be achievable for the millions of workers at the lower end of the economic ladders. These and other barriers in the bill, including the years, often more than a decade that it would take to achieve citizenship make it a flawed piece of legislation and needs to be improved. Until we can pass comprehensive immigration reform we must be aggressive in pursuing policies that are humane and sensible and that keep families together. This includes taking measures that are currently available, including using the presidential power of executive order when it is

appropriate. While the Senate passed the DREAM act
in its immigration bill and while the House has not
acted.I think president Obama did exactly the right
thing through his executive order for Deferred Action
for Childhood Arrivals (DACA). DACA was a good
first step but should be expanded, deferred action
should include the parents of citizens, parents of
permanent legal residents and the parents of
DREAMers. We should be pursuing policies that
unite families, not tear them apart.

Let me now touch on a broader issue which
impacts all Americans but especially lower income
people, whether Latino, African American, White,
Native American, Asian or whatever. And here is the
reality: The reality is that for the last 40 years, the
great middle class of this country has been
disappearing and this has accelerated since the Wall
Street crash of 2008. And while millions of Americans
are working longer hours for lower wages, there is
another reality that we have got to put on the table,
and that is that almost all of the new wealth and
income being created in America today and the last
many years has gone to the top 1% – and that's
wrong. It is not acceptable that we have today the
highest rate of income and wealth inequality at a time
when millions of Americans work longer hours for
lower wages and we have the highest rate of
childhood poverty of any major country on earth. It is
not acceptable that youth unemployment in this

country has reached tragic proportions. The Economic Policy Institute recently told us that if you look at young people from 17 to 20 who are either unemployed or working part time when they want to work full time or have given up looking for work; for white kids that number is 33%, for Hispanic kids it is 36%, for African-American kids it is 51%. That is unacceptable and maybe, just maybe, instead of building more jails and locking up more people, maybe just maybe we should be investing in jobs and education for our young people.

I want America to be known as the country with the best educated population in the world, not the country with the more people in jail than any other country. And that is why I have introduced legislation both for young people and the general population that creates millions of decent paying jobs rebuilding our crumbling infrastructure, transforming our energy system away from fossil fuel. But when we talk about the problems of America it is not only jobs, it is income. We need to raise the minimum wage, which today is a starvation wage of seven and a quarter ($7.25) to 15 bucks ($15) an hour so that anyone who works in this country does not live in poverty. When you talk about the future of America, we talk about the need to compete in a highly competitive global economy and if we are going to compete effectively we need the best educated workforce in the world.

And today in America we have the shameful situation of hundreds of thousands of bright, qualified young people who want to go to college but who can't go to college because their families do not have enough money. That is grossly unfair to those young people and it is grossly unfair and dumb for the future of the American economy and that is why I have introduced legislation which would make public colleges and public universities tuition free. I want to see everyone in this country who has the ability, who has the desire, to be able to get the kinds of education they need and our legislation also deals with the crisis of millions of people struggling under student debt and outrageously high interest rates.

In my view, furthermore, to be a great country our government has got to start protecting working families and not just wealthy campaign contributors and that means policies that end voter suppression. There are politicians who are simply cowardly and are unafraid to face the people because they know their ideas do not represent the majority and the only way they win is by creating situations to make it difficult for people to vote. I want to see us have the highest voter turnout in the world. I want to see us make it easier for people to vote, not harder for people to vote.

The United States is the only major industrialized country that does not guarantee medical and parental

leave for its people. That's wrong. When a woman
has a baby, regardless of her income, she should be
able to stay home with that baby and not be forced to
go back to work.

We need to overturn this disastrous Citizens
United Supreme Court decision which allows
billionaires to buy elections. And brothers and sisters,
we need to create a health care system in this country,
and I'm a strong supporter, I voted for the
Affordable Care Act – but it doesn't go far enough.
Every major industrial country guarantees health care
to all of its people as a right and so should we in the
United States of America.

Let me conclude my remarks by simply saying
this: We are, in America today, the wealthiest country
in the history of the world but most people don't
know that because almost all of the wealth rests in the
hand of the few so what I would like you to do is to
think big, not small. Think of a nation in which every
working parent has quality and affordable child care.
Think of a nation, the wealthiest nation in the history
of the world, where every person regardless of
income can get all the education that they need. Think
of a nation, not where youth unemployment is over
30% but where all of our kids are either in school or
getting good job training or have quality jobs. And
lastly but not leastly, think of a nation where every
person in this country, no matter their race, no matter

their country of origin, no matter their religion, no matter their disability, no matter their sexual orientation, that all of us come together to create the greatest country that anyone has ever seen, a country which works for all of our people and we do it when we stand together and we do not allow people to divide us, divide us, divide us. Thank you all very much.

CHAPTER 9
Waterfront Park Speech
May 26, 2016

"Thank you all very much for being here and for all the support that you have given me over the years: as the mayor of this great city, as Vermont's only congressman and now as a U.S. senator. Thanks also to my longtime friends and fellow Vermonters Bill McKibben, Brenda Torpey, Donna Bailey, Mike O'Day and Ben and Jerry for all that you do – and for your very generous remarks. Thanks also to Jenny Nelson for moderating this event and for your leadership in Vermont agriculture.

I also want to thank my family: My wife Jane, my brother Larry, my children Levi, Heather, Carina and Dave for their love and support, and my seven beautiful grandchildren – Sonny, Cole, Ryleigh, Grayson, Ella, Tess and Dylan who provide so much joy in my life.

Today, here in our small state – a state that has led the nation in so many ways – I am proud to announce my candidacy for president of the United States of America.

Today, with your support and the support of

millions of people throughout this country, we begin a political revolution to transform our country economically, politically, socially and environmentally.

Today, we stand here and say loudly and clearly that; "Enough is enough. This great nation and its government belong to all of the people, and not to a handful of billionaires, their Super-PACs and their lobbyists."

Brothers and sisters: Now is not the time for thinking small. Now is not the time for the same old – same old establishment politics and stale inside-the-beltway ideas.

Now is the time for millions of working families to come together, to revitalize American democracy, to end the collapse of the American middle class and to make certain that our children and grandchildren are able to enjoy a quality of life that brings them health, prosperity, security and joy – and that once again makes the United States the leader in the world in the fight for economic and social justice, for environmental sanity and for a world of peace.

My fellow Americans: This country faces more serious problems today than at any time since the Great Depression and, if you include the planetary crisis of climate change, it may well be that the challenges we face now are direr than any time in our modern history.

Here is my promise to you for this campaign. Not only will I fight to protect the working families of this country, but we're going to build a movement of millions of Americans who are prepared to stand up and fight back. We're going to take this campaign directly to the people – in town meetings, door to door conversations, on street corners and in social media – and that's BernieSanders.com by the way. This week we will be in New Hampshire, Iowa and Minnesota – and that's just the start of a vigorous grassroots campaign.

Let's be clear. This campaign is not about Bernie Sanders. It is not about Hillary Clinton. It is not about Jeb Bush or anyone else. This campaign is about the needs of the American people, and the ideas and proposals that effectively address those needs. As someone who has never run a negative political ad in his life, my campaign will be driven by issues and serious debate; not political gossip, not reckless personal attacks or character assassination. This is what I believe the American people want and deserve. I hope other candidates agree, and I hope the media allows that to happen. Politics in a democratic society should not be treated like a baseball game, a game show or a soap opera. The times are too serious for that.

Let me take a minute to touch on some of the issues that I will be focusing on in the coming months, and then give you an outline of an Agenda for America which will, in fact, deal with these problems and lead us to a better future.

Income and Wealth Inequality: Today, we live in the wealthiest nation in the history of the world but that reality means very little for most of us because almost all of that wealth is owned and controlled by a tiny handful of individuals. In America we now have more income and wealth inequality than any other major country on earth, and the gap between the very rich and everyone is wider than at any time since the 1920s. The issue of wealth and income inequality is the great moral issue of our time, it is the great economic issue of our time and it is the great political issue of our time. And we will address it.

Let me be very clear. There is something profoundly wrong when the top one-tenth of 1 percent owns almost as much wealth as the bottom 90 percent, and when 99 percent of all new income goes to the top 1 percent. There is something profoundly wrong when, in recent years, we have seen a proliferation of millionaires and billionaires at the same time as millions of Americans work longer hours for lower wages and we have the highest rate of childhood poverty of any major country on earth. There is something profoundly wrong when one family owns more wealth than the bottom 130 million Americans. This grotesque level of inequality is immoral. It is bad economics. It is unsustainable. This type of rigged economy is not what America is supposed to be about. This has got to change and, as your president, together we will change it.

Economics: But it is not just income and wealth inequality. It is the tragic reality that for the last 40 years the great middle class of our country – once the envy of the world – has been disappearing. Despite exploding technology and increased worker productivity, median family income is almost $5,000 less than it was in 1999. In Vermont and throughout this country it is not uncommon for people to be working two or three jobs just to cobble together enough income to survive on and some health care benefits.

The truth is that real unemployment is not the 5.4 percent you read in newspapers. It is close to 11 percent if you include those workers who have given up looking for jobs or who are working part time when they want to work full time. Youth unemployment is over 17 percent and African-American youth unemployment is much higher than that. Today, shamefully, we have 45 million people living in poverty, many of whom are working at low-wage jobs. These are the people who struggle every day to find the money to feed their kids, to pay their electric bills and to put gas in the car to get to work. This campaign is about those people and our struggling middle class. It is about creating an economy that works for all, and not just the one percent.

Citizens United: My fellow Americans: Let me be as blunt as I can and tell you what you already know. As a result of the disastrous Supreme Court decision on Citizens United, the American political system has been totally corrupted, and the foundations of American democracy are being undermined. What the Supreme Court essentially said was that it was not good enough for the billionaire class to own much of our economy. They could now own the U.S. government as well. And that is precisely what they are trying to do.

American democracy is not about billionaires being able to buy candidates and elections. It is not about the Koch brothers, Sheldon Adelson and other incredibly wealthy individuals spending billions of dollars to elect candidates who will make the rich richer and everyone else poorer. According to media reports the Koch brothers alone, one family, will spend more money in this election cycle than either the Democratic or Republican parties. This is not democracy. This is oligarchy. In Vermont and at our town meetings we know what American democracy is supposed to be about. It is one person, one vote – with every citizen having an equal say – and no voter suppression. And that's the kind of American political system we have to fight for and will fight for in this campaign.

Climate Change: When we talk about our responsibilities as human beings and as parents, there is nothing more important than leaving this country and the entire planet in a way that is habitable for our kids and grandchildren. The debate is over. The scientific community has spoken in a virtually unanimous voice. Climate change is real. It is caused by human activity and it is already causing devastating problems in the United States and around the world.

The scientists are telling us that if we do not boldly transform our energy system away from fossil fuels and into energy efficiency and sustainable energies, this planet could be five to ten degrees Fahrenheit warmer by the end of this century. This is catastrophic. It will mean more drought, more famine, more rising sea level, more floods, more ocean acidification, more extreme weather disturbances, more disease and more human suffering. We must not, we cannot, and we will not allow that to happen.

It is no secret that there is massive discontent with politics in America today. In the mid-term election in November, 63 percent of Americans did not vote, including 80 percent of young people. Poll after poll tells us that our citizens no longer have confidence in our political institutions and, given the

power of Big Money in the political process, they
have serious doubts about how much their vote
actually matters and whether politicians have any clue
as to what is going on in their lives.

Combatting this political alienation, this cynicism
and this legitimate anger will not be easy. That's for
sure. But that is exactly what, together, we have to do
if we are going to turn this country around – and that
is what this campaign is all about.

And to bring people together we need a simple
and straight-forward progressive agenda which speaks
to the needs of our people, and which provides us
with a vision of a very different America. And what is
that agenda?

Jobs, Jobs, Jobs: It begins with jobs. If we are
truly serious about reversing the decline of the middle
class we need a major federal jobs program which
puts millions of Americans back to work at decent
paying jobs. At a time when our roads, bridges, water
systems, rail and airports are decaying, the most
effective way to rapidly create meaningful jobs is to
rebuild our crumbling infrastructure. That's why I've
introduced legislation which would invest $1 trillion
over 5 years to modernize our country's physical
infrastructure. This legislation would create and
maintain at least 13 million good-paying jobs, while
making our country more productive, efficient and

safe. And I promise you as president I will lead that legislation into law.

I will also continue to oppose our current trade policies. For decades, presidents from both parties have supported trade agreements which have cost us millions of decent paying jobs as corporate America shuts down plants here and moves to low-wage countries. As president, my trade policies will break that cycle of agreements which enrich at the expense of the working people of this country.

Raising Wages: Let us be honest and acknowledge that millions of Americans are now working for totally inadequate wages. The current federal minimum wage of $7.25 an hour is a starvation wage and must be raised. The minimum wage must become a living wage – which means raising it to $15 an hour over the next few years – which is exactly what Los Angeles recently did – and I applaud them for doing that. Our goal as a nation must be to ensure that no full-time worker lives in poverty. Further, we must establish pay equity for women workers. It's unconscionable that women earn 78 cents on the dollar compared to men who perform the same work. We must also end the scandal in which millions of American employees, often earning less than $30,000 a year, work 50 or 60 hours a week – and earn no overtime. And we need paid sick leave and guaranteed vacation time for all.

Addressing Wealth and Income Inequality: This campaign is going to send a message to the billionaire class. And that is: you can't have it all. You can't get huge tax breaks while children in this country go hungry. You can't continue sending our jobs to China while millions are looking for work. You can't hide your profits in the Cayman Islands and other tax havens, while there are massive unmet needs on every corner of this nation. Your greed has got to end. You cannot take advantage of all the benefits of America, if you refuse to accept your responsibilities.

That is why we need a tax system which is fair and progressive, which makes wealthy individuals and profitable corporations begin to pay their fair share of taxes.

Reforming Wall Street: It is time to break up the largest financial institutions in the country. Wall Street cannot continue to be an island unto itself, gambling trillions in risky financial instruments while expecting the public to bail it out. If a bank is too big to fail it is too big to exist. We need a banking system which is part of the job creating productive economy, not a handful of huge banks on Wall Street which engage in reckless and illegal activities.

Campaign Finance Reform: If we are serious about creating jobs, about climate change and the needs of our children and the elderly, we must be deadly serious about campaign finance reform and the need for a constitutional amendment to overturn Citizens United. I have said it before and I'll say it again. I will not nominate any justice to the Supreme Court who has not made it clear that he or she will move to overturn that disastrous decision which is undermining our democracy. Long term, we need to go further and establish public funding of elections.

Reversing Climate Change: The United States must lead the world in reversing climate change. We can do that if we transform our energy system away from fossil fuels, toward energy efficiency and such sustainable energies such as wind, solar, geo-thermal and bio-mass. Millions of homes and buildings need to be weatherized, our transportation system needs to be energy efficient, and we need a tax on carbon to accelerate the transition away from fossil fuel.

Health Care for All: The United States remains the only major country on earth that does not guarantee health care for all as a right. Despite the modest gains of the Affordable Care Act, 35 million Americans continue to lack health insurance and many more are under-insured. Yet, we continue paying far more per capita for health care than any other nation. The United States must join the rest of the industrialized world and guarantee health care to all as a right by moving toward a Medicare-for-All single-payer system.

Protecting Our Most Vulnerable: At a time when millions of Americans are struggling to keep their heads above water economically, at a time when senior poverty is increasing, at a time when millions of kids are living in dire poverty, my Republican colleagues, as part of their recently-passed budget, are trying to make a terrible situation even worse. If you can believe it, the Republican budget throws 27 million Americans off health insurance, makes drastic cuts in Medicare, throws millions of low-income Americans, including pregnant women off of nutrition programs, and makes it harder for working-class families to afford college or put their kids in the Head Start program. And then, to add insult to injury, they provide huge tax breaks for the very wealthiest families in this country while they raise taxes on working families.

Well, let me tell my Republican colleagues that I respectfully disagree with their approach. Instead of cutting Social Security, we're going to expand Social Security benefits. Instead of cutting Head Start and child care, we are going to move to a universal pre-K system for all the children of this country. As Franklin Delano Roosevelt reminded us, a nation's greatness is judged not by what it provides to the most well-off, but how it treats the people most in need. And that's the kind of nation we must become.

College for All: And when we talk about

education, let me be very clear. In a highly competitive global economy, we need the best educated workforce we can create. It is insane and counter-productive to the best interests of our country, that hundreds of thousands of bright young people cannot afford to go to college, and that millions of others leave school with a mountain of debt that burdens them for decades. That must end. That is why, as president, I will fight to make tuition in public colleges and universities free, as well as substantially lower interest rates on student loans.

War and Peace: As everybody knows, we live in a difficult and dangerous world, and there are people out there who want to do us harm. As president, I will defend this nation – but I will do it responsibly. As a member of Congress I voted against the war in Iraq, and that was the right vote. I am vigorously opposed to an endless war in the Middle East – a war which is unwise and unnecessary. We must be vigorous in combatting terrorism and defeating ISIS, but we should not have to bear that burden alone. We must be part of an international coalition, led by Muslim nations, that can not only defeat ISIS but begin the process of creating conditions for a lasting peace.

As some of you know, I was born in a far-away land called Brooklyn, New York. My father came to this country from Poland without a penny in his pocket and without much of an education. My mother graduated high school in New York City. My father worked for almost his entire life as a paint salesman and we were solidly lower-middle class. My parents, brother and I lived in a small rent-controlled apartment. My mother's dream was to move out of that small apartment into a home of our own. She died young and her dream was never fulfilled. As a kid I learned, in many, many ways, what lack of money means to a family. That's a lesson I have never forgotten.

I have seen the promise of America in my own life. My parents would have never dreamed that their son would be a U.S. Senator, let alone run for president. But for too many of our fellow Americans, the dream of progress and opportunity is being denied by the grind of an economy that funnels all the wealth to the top.

And to those who say we cannot restore the dream, I say just look where we are standing. This beautiful place was once an unsightly rail yard that served no public purpose and was an eyesore. As mayor, I worked with the people of Burlington to help turn this waterfront into the beautiful people-oriented public space it is today. We took the fight to the courts, to the legislature and to the people. And we won.

The lesson to be learned is that when people stand together, and are prepared to fight back, there is nothing that can't be accomplished.

We can live in a country:

Where every person has health care as a right, not a privilege;

Where every parent can have quality and affordable childcare and where all of our qualified young people, regardless of income, can go to college;

Where every senior can live in dignity and security, and not be forced to choose between their medicine or their food;

Where every veteran who defends this nation gets the quality health care and benefits they have earned and receives the respect they deserve;

Where every person, no matter their race, their religion, their disability or their sexual orientation realizes the full promise of equality that is our birthright as Americans.

That is the nation we can build together, and I ask you to join me in this campaign to build a future that works for all of us, and not just the few on top.

Thank you, and on this beautiful day on the shore of Lake Champlain, I welcome you aboard."

About the author

Bernie Sanders was elected to the U.S. Senate in 2006 after serving 16 years in the House of Representatives. He is the longest serving independent member of Congress in American history. Born in Brooklyn, Bernie was the younger of two sons in a modest-income family. After graduation from the University of Chicago in 1964, he moved to the Green Mountain State. Early in his career, Sanders was director of the American People's Historical Society. Elected Mayor of Burlington by 12 votes in 1981, he served four terms. Before his 1990 election as Vermont's at-large member in Congress, Sanders lectured at the John F. Kennedy School of Government at Harvard and at Hamilton College in upstate New York.

The Almanac of American Politics has called Sanders a "practical' and "successful legislator." He has focused on the shrinking middle class and widening income gap in America that is greater than at any time since the Great Depression. Other priorities include reversing global warming, universal health care, fair trade policies, supporting veterans and preserving family farms. He serves on five Senate committees: Budget; Veterans; Energy; Environment; and Health, Education, Labor and Pensions.

Made in the USA
Middletown, DE
13 August 2022

71308103R00094